A GEAR HIGHER

THE BICYCLE RACER'S HANDBOOK OF TECHNIQUES

by Keith Code and David Gordon

First Edition

Code Break

ACKNOWLEDGEMENTS

Editors
Su Falcon
Judy Code

Design & Illustration
Peter Green Studios
Brian McLaughlin

Photography
Nelson Machin
Jim Safford
Scott Smith
Chris Chenard

Help and Encouragement
Tireless Testers -
    Kenny Fritts
    Colin Bailey
    Josh Ward
    Larry Longo
    April Lawyer
    Josh Kahle
Marla Streb-Enthusiasm
L. Ron Hubbard-How to Know

Warning: Riding and racing bicycles is both fascinating and exhilarating, partially due to the fact that you risk injury or death by your own or other's errors and actions while doing it. This book is not intended to nor does it claim to remove any of the potential dangers of riding bicycles. It is in fact possible that reading and applying this material could lead to increased exposure to any or all of the potential dangers of riding bicycles. This book contains a written account of observations made by the author and others based on their personal experience. The author and others acknowledge the fact that they have ignored or were possibly unaware of dangers to themselves and may have been in the position to observe these things only because they knew it was dangerous and even desired that danger and accept no responsibility for your individual application of the contents of this book which might result in any harm, injury or property damage to yourself and others. If expert assistance is required, the services of a qualified Cycling Federation coach should be sought.

Always wear protective gear and observe local laws and courtesies.

Printed in the United States of America

Published by
Code Break
Glendale, CA
818-246-0717

ISBN:0-9650450-0-5

A GEAR HIGHER

CONTENTS

SCOTT SMITH

I must say, after I first read Keith Code's A GEAR HIGHER *I felt cheated. I had to learn many of these riding techniques and concepts the hard way! If only I could have picked this book up when I first started racing mountain bikes.* A GEAR HIGHER *is here and I hope other riders can apply Keith Code's clever concepts to help them go smoothly faster... other riders except my competition, that is. —Marla Streb*

This book is based on a simple idea. The idea is that riders only have two commodities to spend and they are both consumable: **physical energy** and **attention**; and they are very similar in some respects.

In life, energy and attention are like money: if we spend too much on one thing we don't have enough to buy or do the other important things. On a bicycle, a rider may spend a little bit of attention on everything he or she does. Let's say you have $10.00 worth of it (attention) to spend.

Trying to get your feet into the clips or clipless pedals the first time you used them probably did not take too much physical energy but it no doubt consumed about $9.90 of your $10.00 worth of attention. As riders progress, things cost them less attention to do; they are able to reduce the costs of things like getting into the clips or cleats to a dime or a quarter. That's a big savings and you can easily mock up what it would be like now if you always had to

spend that original $9.90 every time you wanted to get into the pedals. Not good.

Other things about riding can be reduced to a minimum cost of attention. Everyone has been in the position where they were late making a gear change for some particular hill. Whatever the distractions were, the fact is they consumed enough attention to make the rider forget that gear change—at the exact time it was needed. It wasn't physical energy they were short on—it was attention.

This, then, is one valid way to look at your riding, from the perspective of attention, and how much each action costs. The techniques in this book are intended to help reduce them to a minimum so you have some left over. That spare change is your gateway to improvement. Spend your $10.00 wisely.

Keith Code

Cool compressions or crossings can thrill you when you're flying and then you forget to downshift.

Co-author's note:

Originally, Man began to advance himself through the master/disciple, craftsman/apprentice type of relationship, each new generation improving on the last. Each school of thought and craft from antiquity has blossomed into many offshoot technologies which fashion and improve our abilities and materials. For example, a modern day blacksmith works with computer-guided lasers and machine tools rather than an open fire and hammer.

Bicycling was Man's first personal wheeled sport which did not rely on other creatures to propel it. Motorcycling evolved out of that and has taken the two-wheeled vehicle to an unimaginably high level of sophistication. Machines capable of hurtling over dirt at over 100 MPH, and 200 MPH on paved surfaces, all with fingertip controls, was beyond fiction at the inception of the first bicycle.

While the science and technology involved in building these machines and bicycles balloon our libraries, written material on how to control them wouldn't even fill a supermarket shopping cart.

During my bicycle racing career I found one such book, *A Twist of the Wrist*, written by a man named Keith Code. The concepts and ideas he discovered for motorcycling immediately improved my abilities as a bicyclist and I was able to translate my successes into coaching other riders. My results were improved, as were my students', many of whom went on to win national and world championships based on my interpretation of his ideas and techniques.

Seeing mine and others' success with the material, I immediately wanted to do a full adaptation of his work to bicycling and later, as I came to find out, Code's original book had found its way into many top bicycle competitor's and coaches' libraries.

After proposing the project to Keith and after four years of fascinating research by both of us, we are proud to present a book that will improve your riding. All you have to do now is read and apply the material. If you do, you will improve.

David Gordon

My trainer said, "Don't let the gears take over, take over the gears." That's how I get over the next hill.

I started racing because it was fun, then "accidentally" won a race. From then on, winning was my goal. I realized that sometimes the barrier is not realizing you have a goal, but you always do.

You might not think of resistance as the payout for all your work; but it really is positive feedback, you can count on it and strive to overcome it.

This book is about the subtleties and the barriers of riding. Ignorance of these things is a barrier in itself.

After reading and applying this book I don't say things like, "Darn, I crashed." I have a way of figuring it out.

Riding a bicycle is all about conquering force. Riders use force and the barriers it presents to gauge themselves and their progress: wind resistance, gravity, cornering, rough terrain, distance and speed. All represent something to either overcome or achieve, and force is the apparent barrier AND the weapon of choice to approach them.

This book contains information about a number of things which riders experience when confronted with different kinds of force and it's about how to cheat those forces out of their power to catch riders unaware and thwart their targets and goals.

With force as the main barrier, targets and goals set to overcome it are important to have, whether they be large or small goals, long term or short term any target or goal that a rider has decided to accomplish is valid—pulling a particular hill one gear higher, beating another rider—event, career or purely personal achievements.

Every time a rider bothers to try, there is some target or goal in mind and every goal comes complete with its own set of barriers; every one of them defined by some kind of force. That force may be a physical barrier or, like a goal, exclusively in one's mind.

The harder you try, the more resistance you experience, both internally and externally. That's the good news, because, through your skill, technique, training and better machine components, you have gained access, or figured out how to experience more force and resistance. That's the payout, that's the perk, it's what we get for our efforts.

This material is about defining and overcoming some of the barriers you may have encountered connected with experiencing more force.

Keith Code

A GEAR HIGHER

CHAPTER ONE

The Surface You Ride

Mysteries of the Riding Surface Revealed

Riders invariably have their favorite sections of road or trail and track riders their favorite velodrome—the places where things flow together into a dance and everything happens just the way it's supposed to, with no surprises, and plenty of **attention** to spare.

Why are these routes and places so comfortable? How much should be known about the terrain or road? Which aspects are important and which are not? Why are some sections harder to ride than others?

Before I knew what surfaces really were, it was a mess. I just wanted to go fast. The result? Blown turns—I was thwarted by my own ignorance.

A race course is designed to challenge riding skill. Figuring out what the designer intended can give you a tactical advantage.

Streets and Roads

Streets and roads are constructed so motorists can travel from point A to point B easily. The highway engineers are very considerate; they want to see us make it in one piece so turns are often gently banked.[1] Decreasing-radius[2] corners are rare, and seldom is there a hairpin[3] at the end of a straight stretch of road. Off-camber[4] turns are avoided when-

---

1 When the tilt of the outside riding surface is higher than the inside, this is called banking.
2 A decreasing-radius turn tightens as you go through it.
3 A slow speed, very tight and generally U-shaped turn.
4 The tilt of the outside of the riding surface is lower than the inside.

ever possible and corners are generally constructed in a predictable and straightforward manner.

On the other hand, a road course designer[5] may assemble the corners so that very little, if anything, is done for safety or convenience. Such course setters will purposely design one that excites the spectators, creating changing and challenging situations for riders at the same time. Hairpins are put into the most difficult sections, usually after the fastest straights, and S-turns often have a slower exit than entry. The designer may locate and include corners which baffle us with several camber and radius changes to break the flow and force riders into unusual situations. And regardless of the course, the faster we try to negotiate the turns, the more inherently difficult they become.

Dirt and Off Road

Dirt and off-road trails are often subject to the natural vagaries of the terrain and contain a disproportionate number of hairpins and decreasing-radius corners. On mountain access and fire roads, off-camber turns are strategically placed for water runoff. These roads are designed for trucks and maintenance vehicles, certainly not for high-speed, two-wheeled kamikaze pilots.

Single track[6] is another story. Here the course designer has an opportunity to route the rider through all manner of surprises.

Velodromes

Velodromes offer the most consistent riding surface but can still vary greatly: both indoor and outdoor facilities may be constructed of wood or concrete and have surfaces that range from knurled[7] to polished; they may utilize steep or shallow turns and gradual or abrupt transitions onto the straight-aways. Despite certain universal features, velodromes are as varied as their designers.

At first I just liked death-defying situations and the excitement of the terrain. Now that I understand surfaces, I even like the rocky stuff. In fact, I like it the best.

Velodromes are designed so riders can go flat out, but each has its own character. Understanding that character can be the difference between first and fifth.

5 A course setter, the person choosing the race route.
6 Dirt trails, wide enough for only one machine at a time.
7 Small, sharp-edged ridges, providing a better grip.

In contrast to velodromes we have off road. The only consistency on most off road courses is inconsistency. Every turn is different and a rider's ability to quickly and accurately read the surface is a potent weapon in good cornering

When you know how to beat the terrain you will quit being hesitant and conquer it, not before.

Velodrome designers all have the same goal: to permit a cyclist to go flat out the whole way around. But what was the anticipated "flat out" speed when that specific velodrome was first designed? Was it intended for non-cycling activities as well? What strange notions or preferences did the designer favor in his layout?

Whatever a course or track designer's intentions may be, there are only five major changes that can be found or designed into any surface.

Surface Changes

Changes in Camber

- A piece of road or trail can have a **positive camber** or banking, like a velodrome, the inside of the turn is lower than the outside. It can have an "off" or **negative camber** where the inside is higher than the outside. Or the road can be flat. A turn may be designed with one or more camber changes.

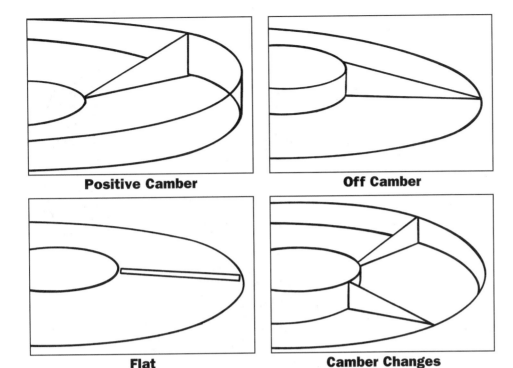

Positive Camber

Off Camber

Flat

Camber Changes

Camber changes are important to recognize. They often dictate the correct approach to a turn.

Changes in Radius

- A single turn may have a constant radius, as in a perfect half circle. It may decrease in radius, tightening up toward the end, or it may have an increasing radius, opening up at the end.

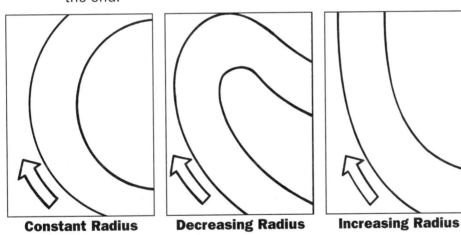

Constant Radius   **Decreasing Radius**   **Increasing Radius**

Not understanding surfaces means you hesitate, means you are tense, means losing your momentum, means you crash.

Series of Turns

- In a series of interdependent turns, the line you take through the initial part of the turn will be partly determined by where you want to exit it and set up for the next turn. A series of turns can have any or all of the camber and radius changes listed above.

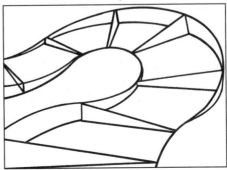

A series of turns can be complicated to ride, especially if you add radius and camber changes to it. The end is usually more important than the beginning.

Elevation can add a third dimension to any camber and radius changes in a turn.

Elevation Changes
- Can be included at any point to any type of turn or change in a road or trail. Elevation changes are **uphill**, **downhill** or **crested** track changes.

Straight Sections
- These are sections where little or no **turning** is required. Increases or decreases in elevation like whoops[8] may be added, and they could also be off camber. These are the five

Straight sections aren't intended to fool you. They simply add length to the course.

Now I find I can even out-descend real road racers by my line selection.

major changes that can be engineered by nature or man into a stretch of road or trail. With the addition of bumpy sections and ruts in the dirt, which may also have been purposely included by a course designer, you have all the possible situations. To understand any turn, its characteristics must first be identified, because each of these changes (except straights) has a direct influence on cornering. **Spending less attention on surface changes, because you understand them, leads to certainty**.

Sweet Spots

On the trail, the surface will vary from hard pack to soft loam and sand, or any combination of these. Techniques that make for fast riding on one surface can land you in the trees on another. On the velodrome, a track rider may find power-spots, places where

---

8 Short for Whoop-de-dos, a succession of two or more low dirt mounds cut across course, or naturally occurring that acts as a series of closely spaced jumps.

he'll feel extra strong, and others which feel "dead" by comparison. The same for a road and off-road courses. It is important to be able to distinguish these spots and know which of the five changes are helping or hurting.

The "wall" created by any banked surface helps you hold your line and go faster.

Positive Camber or Banking

Most everyone is comfortable riding a corner or section of road or trail that has some banking—it has a positive camber. The banking has the effect of holding a bike and rider up by creating a "wall" to push against with the tires. A velodrome is the most extreme example of this, allowing the rider to take what is essentially a hairpin[9] turn at full speed.

On the road or trail it is a little different. You're usually not applying power and the bank slows the bike down when entering the turn because of the increased resistance created by this wall. More technically speaking, gravity is working for us, pulling the rider and bicycle down the wall, counteracting the outward-bound cornering forces.

When you can identify the surface first and then adapt, you can turn anything into a sweet spot.

A **berm** is a section of banked or positive-cambered dirt either purposely constructed to increase corner speed or resulting naturally from the soft dirt of a turn being dug out by rider's wheels. A berm provides two distinct advantages: 1) the bike can be turned quicker, and 2) more speed can be carried into and through the corner than with any other type or combination of the five changes.

The moment you are in the berm you are already in your exit.

It is very difficult to see the banking while riding on it. You may not notice a slight bank at all unless you've looked at the turn before riding it. While riding on even the steepest velodromes and trail berms, the banked sections can actually appear flat while the rest of the world looks like it's been tilted at a 45-degree angle.

---

9 Any relatively tight turn where you exit going in the opposite direction you entered; approximately a one hundred eighty degree turn.

Banking can be deceptive.

Some riders tilt their head to keep it in perspective.

It is easy to be deceived by even a small amount of banking. Because of the leaned over position while cornering riders don't have a straight view of the road. This becomes even more exaggerated as speed is increased.

In the Bank

Once a bank is identified, it's best to design your approach so the banking can be used to its best advantage. Start a banked turn from the outside, very wide. This allows you to be low in the bank, close to the inside of the road or curb at the point where it begins to flatten out, that gives the maximum holding advantage the banking has to offer before beginning to swing wide onto the flatter surface of the turn's exit.

In a turn, The bike and rider combination are just like a weight on the end of a rubber band. The faster it's swung, the heavier the weight becomes from centrifugal force and the wider it swings to the outside. The banking "holds" you in until you move onto the flatter section of road or trail that follows.

Berms can help with late braking because you know you'll be safe when you slam it and hookup.

Riders can go into banked turns faster than would seem possible if they size up a turn exclusively by its radius. This can be

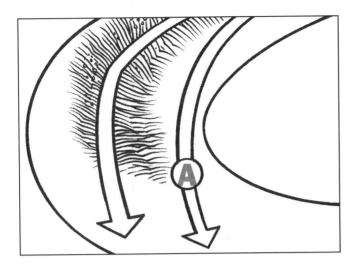

Use the banking to your advantage. (A) A low to the inside line at the exit gives you room to go wider if you need it.

deceptive and riders usually go into them too slowly at first.

Also, when exiting a banked section of road or trail to a flatter surface, a rider must straighten the bike since traction will decrease dramatically when the banking is gone. For example, if you are leaning over all the way, you would have to lean the bike even more in relation to the riding surface to keep that degree of turning radius when the bank is gone. If the bank is ten degrees you must lean it over at least ten more degrees to keep that same turning radius on the flat turn exit surface—which most often can't be done.

Banking provides more pedal clearance than a flat section does, allowing for a much earlier power delivery and a faster acceleration out of this type of turn. If the rider can use it.

Speed Mystery

Riders have been known to ride certain roads and trails very quickly, but when they finally discovered the banked turns in them, they went even faster. Not discovering the banked angles, might lead a rider to believe he is "getting away with" riding speed much higher than normal without a clue as to why. Once a banked section is discovered, it can be used to full advantage.

Negative or Off-Camber Turns

I don't know any riders who regard off-camber turns as their favorites. These turns leave less room for error and definitely do not inspire confidence; they even look wrong to the eye. But unlike banked turns, off-camber ones seem easy to identify, and once understood can become the favorite ones for dusting the competition.

Off Changes

A turn that begins with a bank and ends off-camber demands the most changes and adjustments in lean angles. To continue around it, the bike and rider must continue to lean further in relation to the surface. The effect is much the same as going from a banked to a flat surface. Gravity is now working against the bike/rider combination, pulling it to the outside, reducing pedal clearance and delaying the exit drive. Therefore, good riders set up

Lots of pros are bragging about off-camber turns being their favorites because it takes more skill to ride them.

It is so satisfying to understand a difficult corner and get a smooth pass through it.

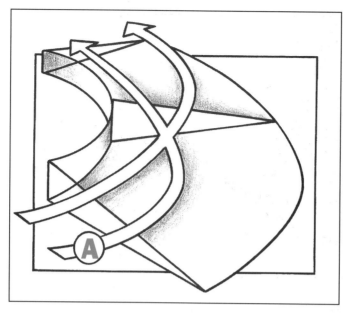

Squaring off (A) is used to handle the bad effects of off-camber or slippery turns.

off-camber turns so they're in the off-camber situation as short a time as possible— the exact opposite of their banked turn strategy— and they certainly don't want to be committed to their maximum lean angle when entering an off-camber section.

An effective plan for off-camber turns is called <u>squaring off</u> the turn. This refers to the type of turn handling that helps lessen the effects of negative camber. Basically, the approach is designed to remain as vertical as possible for as long as possible by choosing an exact spot to dramatically change direction. For example, in a long off-camber section in dirt let the bike swing to the outside, slide the back end around and pick it up to power out of the turn.

In a shorter corner, turn sharply before the off camber then ride directly through it with less lean angle. You might also go straight through the turn as vertically as possible, swing wide toward the exit and make the steering change after the off camber has ended.

Sliding the back end in dirt can get lots of turning done in a short time. This gives a relatively shallow lean angle throughout the rest of the turn and maintains better traction. Sliding on the road is impractical but the same "squared off turn" idea can work there as well, and in slippery conditions.

Your bike setup is more important in off camber: traction is lessened and you almost want a shorter stem to slow down the steering.

Following the fast male pros, I noticed they were squaring off their turns. Patience pays off when you can use it. If you can't, you just go through the ribbon.

Flat Turns

Turns with no negative or positive camber—flat turns—will not increase or decrease the lean angle necessary to negotiate them at a constant radius or speed. Contrary to popular belief, in turns of this kind the fastest way through is usually the tightest line—it's also the shortest distance around the turn. In a flat turn, there is no attempt to fool the rider unless there is a radius change as well. On the trail, a hardpacked straight-away leading into a sandy turn, or vice versa, can introduce some exciting variations to flat turns.

Longer flat turns commit the rider to his maximum lean angle and maximum speed for the longest period of time. Since you'd be riding around the inside at maximum speed and maximum lean sooner or later, you may as well get down to it at the beginning. Taking too wide an entry into most flat turns only gives someone a chance to pass on the inside.

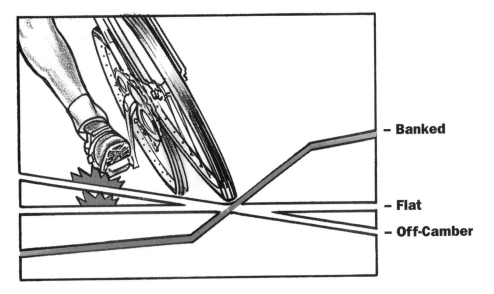

- Banked

- Flat

- Off-Camber

Camber changes dramatically affect how a turn can be ridden. Banked or bermed turns are the only two where you can pedal safely.

Changes in Radius

Turns with changes in their radius will put additional twists in the action. Here are the basic kinds of radii and how to handle each on the road or the trail.

Constant-Radius Turns: A constant-radius (CR for short) turn neither increases (widens) nor decreases (tightens) while going through it. As mentioned above, if it is a fairly long CR turn with no camber changes, you will eventually wind up on the inside of the turn for most of it. In a short turn, riders have other options on how to set up their entries and exits. In a really tight hairpin you must make an abrupt turning change—it should be done at the point at which you feel most confident. There is no set rule as to how it should be done.

If a CR turn has camber changes, it can act as a decreasing-radius (DR) or as an increasing-radius (IR) turn. For example, If the turn is banked on the entry and flattens out on the exit, it will have exactly the same effect on you and your bike as the DR turn. If it's flat on the entry and banked on the exit, it acts as an IR. Here again, knowing the location of the camber changes will help.

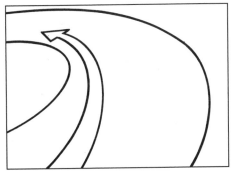

The notorious decreasing radius turn (A) designed to let you in faster than it lets you out. Increasing Radius (B) turns are usually easy to ride, but can be made difficult with camber changes.

Decreasing-Radius

A turn that tightens up is a decreasing-radius (DR) turn. The road or trail can deceive a rider into treating it as a constant-radius turn. If he falls for that, he then must do one of three things: 1) run wide at the exit 2) lean the bike over more at the end of the turn or 3) cut the speed— which helps avoid #1 and #2.

A long decreasing radius turn must be "squared off."

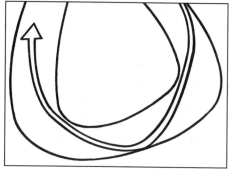

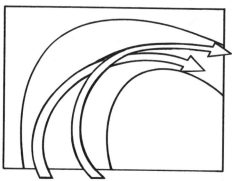

You may be passed using a wide entry line but it is still the most efficient handling for the simple decreasing radius turn.

Squared DR

Some misleading information about handling DR turns has been circulating for years which says that you should "late apex" them. This may be true in a tight DR turn, but in a larger one it must be **double-apexed**. This is another application of the <u>squaring off</u> idea. In a longer DR turn you must ride what is there. What is there is two apexes; try to cheat the turn out of the first one and it will nail your speed down in the second.

Taking a wider and later turn entry line is the standard handling for a simple DR turn. This is the actual approach strategy people call late apexing.

A particularly deceptive type of DR turn is one that is flat on the entrance and banked at the exit. As it will act as an IR or CR turn, depending on the steepness of the banking, a rider's ability to spot these can make a difference in whether or not he gets that half pedal-stroke on the competition it offers him.

Turn Strategy

If a turn is constructed so that it forces you to go slow at some point, you must decide where to go slow instead of letting the turn decide your fate. By figuring a turn correctly, you ride it—it doesn't ride you. If you've made a big mistake in the line, you have probably just been sucked into riding the course the way it looks rather than the way it is, and chances are good that it was a DR turn or had a radius change that made it act like one. *Can you think of an example of this?*

Increasing Radius

Every course has some DR turns and some are off camber. You have to identify them and "admit" to yourself they aren't fast and set up for the exit drive.

An <u>increasing-radius turn</u> (IR) widens, its radius expanding as you go through it. An IR turn gives the safest feeling because there is room at the end to make changes and corrections or drift for tactical reasons; these are the turns that make anyone feel like a pro.

It's rare to make a speed entry error going into an IR turn because there is normally plenty of room to go wide at the end. An IR turn can, however, be changed dramatically by the camber of the road, just as the DR turn can.

If it is banked going in, and flat or off-camber at the exit, it will act as a CR or DR turn, depending upon how much negative camber it has. **Even though the radius of a turn may be its most obvious characteristic, it is often second in importance to its camber changes.**

Series of Turns

Two or more turns linked together in such a way as to influence each other are a <u>series of turns</u>. They're often designed to slow riders down at a place where they otherwise could go faster; sometimes this is done for safety reasons. In a race, on the road or trail, these turns are exciting for the spectator due to the constant slowing and accelerating that bunch up the field and slow the riders so spectators can read the sponsor's patches!

An example of these turns might be where the entry into a two-turn "S" is faster than the exit. However, if the entry is taken as fast as possible, it will spoil the exit. If the entry is approached with the exit in mind, the rider will sacrifice some speed going in for earlier power delivery and improved drive coming out of the turns. This is a better strategy than having to back off in the middle then trying to pedal in some part of the turn, resulting in possible pedal clearances and lean-angle problems, as well as upsetting weight distribution and traction capabilities. It is very distracting to make this kind of change in the second or third turn in a series.

Veteran Strategy

Champions consistently say that you must go slow in some places to go fast in others. Their "slow," of course, would put most of us into cardiac arrest. Here again, the road or trail attempts to lull us into taking action either too soon or too late. In some high-speed S turns, being temperate with speed on the way in and setting up a smooth exit is worth seconds in the corners and is easier on the muscles; this could be the difference between winning and losing.

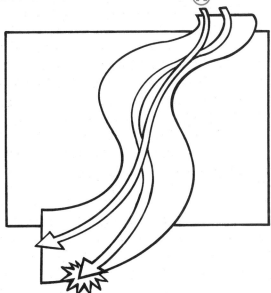

Many mountain roads and trails contain fine examples of these <u>series of turns</u>. As you only spend a short time in turns, often two seconds or less, timing your exit drive is the key to using the old "slow to go fast" concept, not only in S-turns but other turns as well. It works!

Uphill, Downhill and Crested

When a race course contains changes in elevation, it can create some exciting changes in how it must be ridden. <u>Uphill</u> and <u>downhill</u> sections of road or trail don't pose any particular handling

IR turns are forgiving. But you have to see them to use them.

Spending speed in a series of turns is like spending attention. Spend wisely going in (A) and have plenty at the end.

A big cliché in slalom is "running late." It means you are setting up an imaginary turn point 1/2 way to the next gate so you don't run wide.

Prejumping a crest gets you back on the ground and decreases air time so you're in control.

problems unless they are in conjunction with tricky camber changes, radius changes or both. Of course, getting up the hills is another story. Difficulties in rolling hill-type sections usually arise where there is a crest or sharp rise followed by a downhill. At this point, the bike will feel light and be light on the surface.

A turn with a crest in the middle is also tricky because the bike tends to stand up and go toward the outside. Again, there is less traction. It has the same affect as a patch of off-camber road. It is better to go over a crested turn as vertically as possible. The best part of crested sections is; you can get good air.

Brake Up

Braking over a crested hill is tricky because the downward pressure of your bike is lessened—this results in decreased traction. **Hard braking should never be done at a crest; before or after are always the better alternatives.**

Although braking on uphill sections is rare, you have the advantage of gravity pulling you back down the hill, and can therefore slow or stop quicker than on flat or downhill. Braking into a fifteen degree slope gives a 27% improvement in stopping. You can brake 27% harder than on a flat surface without locking up the wheel. On a downhill the situation is reversed; the brakes can lock very easily, dramatically affecting lean angle, traction and steering.

Straight Sections

Straight sections of road or trail with no turns or changes have a different use. Straight-aways are a great place to relax for a bit, check on the competition, have a drink and gather strength for imminent effort, and check to see if breathing is regular. We'll mention this again, but riders often hold their breath during intense riding, which greatly affects their efficiency.

Rest, tuck and you'll go faster on straights. Over 30 mph forget the pedaling, tuck. I picked up 5 seconds at Pikes Peak just with this.

Transitions make the bike either light or heavy. Light coming out of banked or bermed turns, heavy in compressions. This affects traction.

Transitions

On velodromes and other banked surfaces, the contrasting angles of turns to straights produce transitions. The greater the difference and the quicker the change in these angles, the more abrupt the transition. In fact, they act like "crests" where the bike/rider package becomes light on the road surface.

On the velodrome, turning up and down the banking produces situations you must be aware of. Going up, and at slower speeds, results in greatly reduced ground clearance—the outside pedal is very close to the riding surface. The solution is to push the bike away from you toward the inside of the track, more perpendicular to the turn's surface.

Turning down any bank produces a steep descent and will

Using banking for a hill to gain speed is practical but produces a wildly off-camber turn at the bottom.

quickly increase speed. Here, a rider would be using the banking as a hill rather than a surface to counteract outward bound cornering forces. However, while this is a standard and essential strategy to increase velocity and improve or change position, you must turn at some point or run off, and this turning produces a very high G-force load.

Essentially, you'd be straightening the bike in relation to the banking (becoming more perpendicular to the earth) to point it down-track. Now the rider has created an off-camber situation **and** he has high load on the tires. This **transition** produces a very real traction concern.

Power Spots / Dead Spots

While riding, everyone has noticed that some sections of a road or a turn feel exceptionally good for power delivery. They feel free, like gravity took a vacation and wind resistance went on strike; each erg of energy output feels amplified and goes further with no additional effort. Descending a banked section would be the most obvious of these.

Other areas, for no apparent reason, feel the opposite, like pedaling in bubble gum, very dead and unresponsive. Because bicyclists often must make a physical effort, or some other change to handle them: out of the saddle, changing gears, different muscles used, body position on the bike, bar grip and so on, they're probably more aware of these **changing resistances** than athletes in other sports and pay a good deal of attention to them.

This is another reason for understanding the road you ride. For whatever reason these power and dead spots exist, be it mental or physical, a rider's ability to maximize the affects of the power ones and minimize the dead areas can come as a direct result of that understanding.

You know you've beat a section when you are drifting it. Then you shoot for drifting all the turns.

Wrap

The place you ride, whether it be public roads or on the race course, is made up of the five components: camber, radius, elevation changes, series of turns and straights. On the dirt, there are the added variables of solid to loose surfaces, but the general rules apply with added emphasis on sliding and correction. How these components are combined determines your approach to riding them with confidence.

Adding speed tests and re-tests riding skills and strength. Your task is to unravel and identify the five mysteries of the road, trail or velodrome. No amount of bravery will substitute for understanding, and no special bike or equipment will overcome the forces generated by these five components.

Can you use this data in your riding?

CHAPTER TWO

What You Do
You Become A Scientist

This material helped me handle lots of real obvious errors like braking in turns—after I became active at thinking over my races.

The rider's ultimate weapon is his ability to perform the actions of riding <u>and</u> to observe and <u>remember</u> what he has done. But paying enough **attention** to your riding to accurately recall it later can be seen as too much thinking and not enough doing. How does a rider get through the "think" band of riding to the just-do-it level of skill? What are the pitfalls? How do you overcome them?

Rule # 1:
Don't Badmouth Yourself

Many riders have a habit of speaking in negatives about their riding. "I didn't go hard enough; I shouldn't have sprinted out of

Pointing out things you didn't do is impossible to correct. Don't be so hard on yourself.

that one; I don't use the brakes that well, I need to get a better line through this or that turn." Didn't. Can't. Shouldn't have, don't, too much, not enough. Most riders use these negative words much too often. How can information about what you didn't do right, or about things that were almost or not quite done, ever improve anybody's riding? If you're riding at all you are already doing more right than wrong. The job is to accurately identify those correct actions and drop the incorrect ones. **It's a dead-end road to improvement when riders place too much attention on wrongs rather than rights.**

Riders make excuses from what they remember instead of using it to improve.

Rule # 2:
You Can't Correct What You Didn't Do

The only way to make changes and improvements in anyone's riding is to change what was done. To do that they'd have to know exactly what was done, not what wasn't. You didn't do a lot of things on your last ride—you didn't wash your car, you didn't go to church, and you didn't do just about everything else there is to do in life. You only did what you did.

Falling into the **trap** of trying to correct riding by looking at what wasn't done is 180 degrees off any target to improve; it leaves nothing to change. "I didn't brake late enough in that mean hairpin," sounds innocent enough, but what information does it contain to help a rider improve? If he said instead, "I started braking at the big rock just before the last tree on the left, and now I know I can brake even later than that," he knows what was done and now has something to constructively build on.

It's simple—think of riding in negatives and there is nothing to change—look at it the way it actually was and there is something to change. **Changing something you didn't do is impossible.**

Too many riders think of things as being out of their hands, just luck, but even flats can be avoided if you remember the sections and set your bike up correctly.

Unmaze Yourself

Thinking negatively about riding puts anyone in a maze. A mirror maze works like that—it offers no beginning point to start thinking from, then disorients the person by covering up where he's been and where he can go. There is no reckoning point and too many possibilities.

When there is a firm idea of where you came from you can always go back to that point in your mind and look it over. It's the same with riding techniques and control operations. Knowing what was done gives a stable base from which to make corrections the next time out. **Riding is one thing—riding plus being aware of what you are doing is quite another.**

You have only so much attention to spend on what you are doing—your ten dollar bill. If it's spent all on just riding and none on observing what's being done, you can still go quite fast. But spending nine dollars on riding and one on observing the actual riding actions you're doing, gives something to look at and change when off the bike. Hoping to work yourself into a fever pitch won't be necessary—you can go faster by figuring out how to do it better.

Using mistakes to learn, not for excuses about why you couldn't do it, works!

Rule # 3:
Fifty-One Percent

20/20 hindsight and observing what is being done are two different breeds of cat. In the first, a rider would reflect on what he coulda, shoulda or woulda done. That's another variety of violation of rule #2 and is a mental dead end as well. Badmouthing yourself (rule # 1) is worse so the fifty-one percent rule is your only hope. It goes like this.

Doing a little bit more right than wrong, maybe not every time out but consistently, is winning the improvement game. Fifty-one percent every time eventually accumulates to one hundred percent of anyone's capability. **No matter how slight, any observed improvement is improvement, period.**

Getting the bike to drift and not to brake in turns are big things but subtle as well. As you go along, you start to look for more subtle changes that lead to improvements.

Recapture the feeling. Thinking it over after you ride pays big dividends in skill.

I set goals for things like gate starts and on a daily basis I might work on my spin. Once you start looking for improvements you start to see more areas you can improve.

Riders may notice they had some free attention in a complicated area, went a tiny bit faster through a difficult section, read the competition more accurately, had a slight time improvement, remembered to breathe, felt good about something, had fun, didn't tense up, were in control, recognized a surface change and so on and on. The smallest observed change can open the door for more.

This is not to say there will never be a bad day, but look at rule number one for directions on how to handle it.

Observation Payback

How does a rider develop this wonderful ability to ride and observe what he's doing at the same time? **He simply decides to do it.** Make an effort to look at what you are doing while doing it. Try it. If you already have a record of your best times or section times on the trail, closed road course or velodrome, go out the next time and make an effort to observe yourself riding.

Recording turns and difficult sections for future reference can be valuable. You use the information later.

The first thing you'll notice will be that you went slower while doing both the riding and observing. It costs a lot of attention to do both things at once and you won't be willing to ride as hard while doing it. Don't give up. You're spending a lot on looking and a little less on doing.

Take a mental note of course layout and lines so you can just race at race time.

Attention Drill

1. Take an entire training session on the bike to observe every possible detail of what is happening.
2. After riding, think over the observations you made.
3. The next time out, just ride, don't think.

You are faster in the long run when you have taken the time to observe what is needed.

You'll notice one of two things: a) you went faster, or b) the riding became less work than before. It's also possible that both things happened—you went faster with less effort.

I now do this attention drill all of the time.

An accurate mental recording of what you do on the bike while on course is invaluable.

Attention Trap

Riding with less mental effort means more attention is being spent on what's important and less on just being ready for surprises. Not knowing what's coming up in a turn, for example, will create tension. If a rider has taken some time to observe, he'll spend less attention on possible surprises. The mind rules the body. Less mental effort translates directly to reducing physical stress.

Attention Sponge

Mental effort comes disguised in other forms as well. For example, it may take some time for a rider to decide it's okay to slide a bit in the turns, especially on the road. Until then, a rider will be spending a good deal of attention on **trying not to slide**. And herein lies another key: It costs more attention to keep something from happening than it does to make something happen.

The tenseness in most riders' "styles" is a result of their being ready for the worst. Their attention is on something which isn't actually happening. Observing where and what happened will make something like a little rear wheel slide or tricky set of gear changes less of a black hole for your attention.

Lucky Socks

Riders who just ride and don't observe believe that everything that happened to them, both physically and mentally, must be reproduced exactly and in the same order for them to repeat a good performance. This is one of the ways riders become superstitious.

Because he doesn't know exactly what helped, a rider may go about trying to keep all factors the same as they were at the time he rode well, lucky socks and all. You *can* keep things the same, but only by observing what was done and by deciding which factors worked best. This will greatly free attention from those things that were not crucial to improvement. Observing what was done, not the socks you wear, is the key to learning by mistakes.

Let it Go

Riders can easily cheat themselves out of the knowledge to be gained from mistakes. Let's say you got into a turn a little fast and went wide, off your line. Normally, you would try to get back to that good line—to what worked before. That's fine, but there's a twist. If someone "rides out their mistake," they will learn how that different line works. Trying desperately to get back to the ideal once an error has been made won't tell you anything except that a mistake was made. Riding out that mistake gives valuable information about how to handle it should it ever happen again.

Everything a rider does may be a little wrong, but at least they should know what happened—and that's the starting point for change. Riders have been known to adapt a completely new method of riding after making mistakes. Ride out your mistake and see what happens. As above, it will always cost more attention and effort to try to keep something from happening than to go through with what's been started.

You want to know the course just as well as you know the refrain to your favorite song.

That first turn at Mammoth used to do this to me. All my attention was on not crashing and falling over the cliff. I conquered it by simply noting where I had my attention spent.

I used to eat 4 pieces of aged red licorice and 1 fireball exactly 10 minutes before each race. I was stressed without it!

From the candy I went to purposely crashing before the race... it relaxed me.

Drop the mistakes during a race because you'll try and make up for them and race way faster than you practiced (try to).

Too Late

Another way of viewing this is: **By the time a mistake is made it's too late to correct it.** This is one piece of conventional wisdom which is true. Once a mistake occurs at any time, in any turn, the clock can't be rolled back nor can the ground you've already covered. Figure out what was done and correct it the next time out. The root of any mistake is the control change or decisions made and acted upon just before the problem occurred. Here again, rule # 1: Don't badmouth yourself for the error.

A good example of this is going into a DR turn and being way wide in the middle. A rider gets there because it was where he had pointed the bike the last time he made a steering change. Most riders would say, "I didn't turn deep enough." That isn't true. Actually, he turned it in too early.

"I blew the berm," really means you chose the wrong speed or line.

Why

It will take even longer for the rider to realize what happened if he begins looking for the problem from when he first noticed it ("I went wide in that turn") than if he goes back to the earlier point before he began the turn. He has to realize that he was operating from an earlier decision "to go in low and straight." It might have been the result of a bump or slippery patch which momentarily caught his attention. Whatever the reason may be: **If you decide upon the wrong explanation for a mis-**

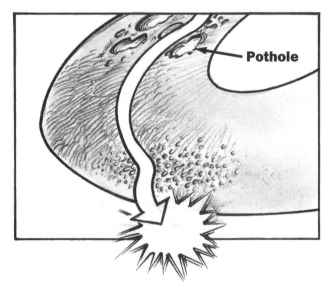

Pothole

Recalling where you spent your attention will give you a reason why a mistake happened. Understanding the exact problem leads to the right solution.

take, the solutions for it will also be wrong. This is another basic reason for being a careful observer of **what you do**.

Being able to ride is important, but riding and observing leads to understanding. *Can you think with this?*

CHAPTER THREE

The Product

Developing Precision With Understanding

What is a line? What is the best line through any corner? Why is one rider's line and style different from another?

100 Years of Improvement

Gigantic strides in machine technology have been made in the last one hundred years of cycling—not to mention physical conditioning, strength and power-gaining methods. All of this equals greater speed. However, not much attention has been spent on the correct procedures for directing all of this technology through turns in the most efficient manner.

A line is the space you use to go through a turn. All of them work. Which one is yours?

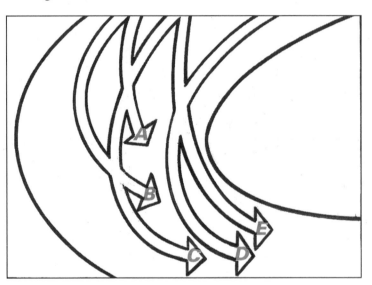

Your Line

A rider's **line** could be described as the <u>exact</u> real estate used to negotiate a turn, his path of progress or an imaginary line that follows or defines that path, from the turn's beginning to its end.

Lines used to be done in two ways:
1. Copy where the lead guy went. He did what was done before him, etc., and that "tradition" is still followed for pack riding.
2. In theory, for a motorcycle, car or bicycle, it was reckoned that the straightest line through the turn was the fastest line.

This is not necessarily true today: physics and natural laws have not changed; but almost every mechanical facet of bicycles has been hit by the tech attack, allowing any rider more line freedom.

Old Line, New Line

The old-timers had to take the smoothest, straightest, shortest line through the turns because their bikes were both heavy and fragile. Abrupt changes in direction, braking on rough or rippled surfaces, over-enthusiastic braking while leaning over and other current day riding possibilities were out of the question. If someone took an average Category One rider of today and an "off the floor" 1990's racing bike back to the very rough Paris-Roubaix race in 1950, he'd probably win simply on machine superiority, and his ability to choose lines would be a major factor.

Product

A product is something which is produced; it is the end result when all the work is done. A product is what can be observed as a result—or held in the mind. You can turn it over to see if it can be produced better or differently, whether it should be corrected or left alone.

A turn or series of turns has a "product." It is that point where you can say, "I'm done with that turn—here's what I did this time, here's what happened. Now what can I do to improve it?" The simplest way to recognize that spot is to remember where you were brave enough to think, "I could go through that one quicker." **The moment your attention is free to review a turn, you're done with it.**

At that point, the sum total of everything done in the turn is neatly wrapped up; what was done either worked or it didn't. Some parts of the product were assembled correctly, maybe some weren't. This product has a location which, for example, might be a point three feet from the outside edge, just next to "that patch" of asphalt or right past the big rock coming out of that hairpin. This known space on the course now becomes a wealth of information for those who can use it.

One level of product is: optimal speed and time through the turn, feeling in control of the turn, not stressed and with the line correct for the next section.

Other Factors

Other factors, besides the bike's location on the road, track or trail, are important parts of the product called **sub-products**:

1. The gear you're in.
2. Your speed at that point.
3. Your body position.
4. Weight distribution on the bike.
5. Degree of lean angle.
6. The amount of control you have over the bike.
7. The steering action you are or are not taking.
8. Delivery of your power.
9. Tire traction.
10. Your impression of what you did and how well it worked out.
11. A comparison of this pass through the turn with earlier passes.

All of these and possibly more are part of the product for that turn. **The quality of your product is determined by all of what happened and how it worked.**

Sometimes the fastest line isn't safe so you have to gauge your chance of making it and your own confidence.

The product of a turn is what you have at the end. It's what you did and how it all worked.

1
2
3
4
5
6
7
8
9
10
11

I have "mud lines," "dry lines" and "guy lines" (which require extra upper body strength) and also "fatigue lines" for when I'm tired.

Sub-Products

Each of the above are called sub-products: a definite set of <u>known circumstances or actions which lead to the product</u> for that turn, and each has a location on the course or track. There are, however, no universal correct products or sub-products; they vary from rider to rider based on ability. Your product is a known destination along a known route. You should know where you're going on the bike and the course, and the product is the place and circumstances you're going for.

The rider with the best product goes the fastest through and out of the turns with the least effort, both physically and mentally. The products and sub-products are the result of a predetermined and pre-decided **plan of action**, based upon the rider's knowledge and abilities.

There's a lot more to the product of a turn than I thought. It's the details, not just whether or not it felt good or bad to you.

End back to beginning.

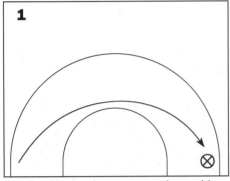

The Product is where you are done with the turn. It is a place you know.

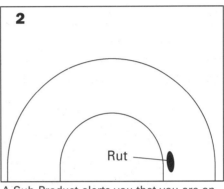

A Sub-Product alerts you that you are on the right track to your Product. You see it.

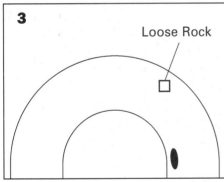

You locate another Sub-Product or Reference Point to guide you through the turn.

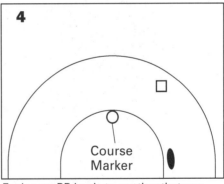

Each new RP leads to another that you know is going to be there.

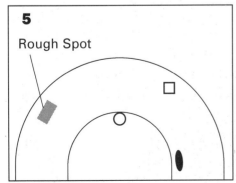

You build confidence by knowing where you are on the track.

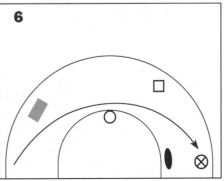

You become able to "see" the turn before you even begin to go through it.

We used radar and found some riders were 10 mph faster going in but way slower coming out. Your product is what counts.

Your Line Is Your Plan

Early on I figured that a fast rider had the right line. If it were that simple, everyone would be fast.

From talking to most riders, it is easy to believe that once they find the "right line" for a turn, everything will magically turn out OK and their times around the course will improve because of this knowledge. It isn't true.

A coach can show a rider the "right line" around a race course. He can even have a rider follow him for laps, or down the same trail repeatedly, copying the motions at moderate speeds. But when the rider rides the course or trail on his own, he'll still bring his own individual touch to the ride—it's almost impossible for him not to. This phenomena has been observed with riders and their coaches all over the world.

Many riders have placed themselves in the same situation, asking champions to show them their "lines" around preset road

At 6´4˝ and 200 lbs. his plan is different than yours—following him would be impossible for most riders.

Everyone has their secret lines during practice but everyone sees them in the semis and then they try to run them in the main with no practice.

Running someone else's lines does not automatically make you faster.

I started with one strong point—I was fearless—no skills at all. I preferred fast, treacherous courses.

courses, downhill mountain bike trails, and various velodromes. They followed in the hopes of finding out some deep, dark riding secrets.

They did find out. They found out that **a rider's line** is **his plan** for going through a turn. His **plan** is based on what he does well and what he doesn't do well. Any rider's **plan** will be based upon <u>his or her</u> own strengths and weaknesses. A line is the result of how each rider's strengths and weaknesses fit together.

For example, riders who use the maximum amount of lean angle the bike and tires have to offer will usually design their "line" to use lots of it. Their line is a lower turn entry, often tight to the inside. By contrast, a rider who does not use all of the tire traction available to him will design his line (plan) so that he does not have to spend so much time leaned over to the maximum: he must try to finish his steering quickly, straighten the bike and crank out of the turn. **All riders intuitively design their turns around what they believe to be their strongest skills.** *What are your strongest skills?*

Learning a Line

Following another rider can be very instructional <u>if</u> his plan can be determined by watching him. If his plan is better designed to handle a turn than yours, and you can see why it is better, you may learn how to use your own abilities to more efficiently handle some other riding situations—or even learn how to counter his plan. **The true value in following another rider, other than drafting,**[10] **is in understanding his plan and being able to expand your own riding because of it.** It's not learning the line; it is learning the **plan** that counts. Observing other riders' plans, products and sub-products to fit them into your racing strategy and riding style to best advantage, is another facet of being able to observe what you do.

Copycat

Following requires a high level of skill. When anyone can do his own job, watch the other rider doing his, remember what the other rider did plus what he did and how it worked out; and when you consider that your own riding usually takes all of your attention, it's quite a juggling act.

Riders often oversimplify this by attempting to look like another, more skilled rider; adopting some obvious characteristic of the other's riding, like body position on the bike. There is nothing wrong with being a copycat, it can lead to understanding the other rider's plan and product—if it can be done. *Have you observed another rider's plan and made it work for you?*

Basic Goal

A basic goal in any turn would be finding the earliest possible acceleration point out of the turn to carry speed to the next one, up a hill, or down the straight in the shortest amount of time with the greatest speed and least effort. Yet it is common for riders to come out of a turn with more effort and harder acceleration than before without decreasing the time because their corner speed was low. This can be deceptive.

Turn Balancing

Getting the best product from a turn requires turn balancing: balancing acceleration out of the turn against the amount of time it takes to get through it. The most common mistake riders make is to go into turns faster and faster, then come out of them at the same speed or slower. It's easier to go into a turn faster than it is to come out faster.

Going in too fast can cost a rider his exit setup and mph coming out. It's important to be able to carry a faster entrance speed through to the exit of the turn to improve overall time. Going in too fast then fouling up in the middle of the turn will lower the exit speed by reducing your momentum[11] and control.

Turn balancing is like your ten dollars worth of attention. Figure that there are only so many miles per hour to spend in a turn on any particular lap for any particular line. If mph are spent

Gaining strength and stamina helped make up for lack of skill, NOT. I just powered out of turns—after blowing most of them!

I once watched Miles Rockwell descend at Vail before the national. I then pretended that I was he. It worked! That was my smoothest and fastest section.

The radar gun example above was the final lesson I needed to learn on this idea of turn balancing.

---

10 To drive close behind another vehicle to take advantage of the reduced air pressure in the wake of the leading vehicle.

11 Force or speed of movement

unwisely at the beginning of the turn, they aren't there at the end. **Excess speed at the wrong time costs time.**

Lots of lines may work, but it usually doesn't pay to jump at the first opportunity to go faster. The increased speed at the exit of one turn will be added to the speed carried all the way to the next.

Slow In, Fast Out

So, higher entry speed isn't always the answer. For example, in a decreasing radius turn, going in a bit slower, but on a line that allows you to start acceleration sooner, can sometimes more than make up for the slightly slower entrance speed.

On the other hand, the speed that wasn't scrubbed off with brakes or with cornering resistance has already been paid for, now it's free! The more of it that's kept through the turn's midsection the cheaper it is to get down to the next turn quicker.

Both ideas have merit, depending on the turn. Trying for a high entry speed into a paved hairpin is generally foolish. Getting

A low line into a DR turn may be fast at first. Which plan do you like?

In hairpins you are going to almost be at a dead stop anyhow so you can go in as fast as possible and late brake.

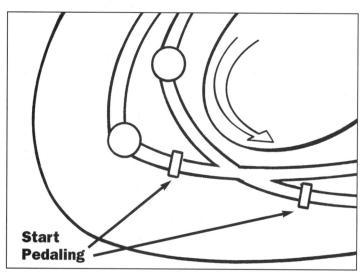

Start Pedaling

into it, turned, and back to the pedals early, is more to the point. Longer, faster turns are the opposite. A little more entry speed will carry the bike through the nonpedaling portion to a greater advantage. The old adage is: **Go fast in fast turns, slow in the slow ones.** That's good advice.

One mph faster in a tight hairpin may gain 1/100th of a second whereas in a longer turn it can make ten times that or more. Use the idea of **turn balancing** to produce the correct product: **Quickest time through the turn; the earliest possible power delivery with good control and positioning of the bike.**

Find the Product

How do you find the product? Let's assume a rider has ridden the course a few times and has figured out what the course designer has in store for him. He's studied the radius changes, the camber changes and the type of surface. He has properly been suspicious of the turns on the course knowing they're meant to challenge and fool him. With this information he should have a good idea of how every turn can affect him and the bike.

I began to give my training more thought once I found I could break a turn down scientifically.

A product is built by applying that information to the observations made while riding. For example, you notice you were late getting back to the power at the exit of a turn. You recall that the bike was still sliding—you were too wide to start pedaling—the bike was still leaning too far. The turn is a little off-camber to the outside in the middle.

The solution would be to use less entry speed to keep from going so wide into the off-camber section, square off the corner by picking a slide point to get it turned, then back into the pedals early. Looking at it from the **end back to beginning**, now there is a starting point and places on the course to work with, correct, change and make decisions about.

My physical training was always scientific, now, so is my cornering. I can break a turn down into a little package of data.

Product Map

Having a product in mind for a turn is like having a road map and a destination for a trip. You'd have a very hard time getting to your destination if you didn't know where it was. It's difficult to get from New York to Kansas City unless Kansas City's whereabouts is known, and a race or a breakaway can't be lead if a rider doesn't know where the course leads! Obtaining a precise product for a turn is the first step in deciding how to improve. *Having no product is really like having no destination in mind.*

This process does not have to be laborious and tedious, indeed, many riders are able to achieve it after only a brief course acquaintance. It is a valuable tool to be used to handle barriers or when things are not improving up to expectations. Do you have an ideal in mind for this section? Exactly what isn't working? Which particular part of the section is snagging your attention? What don't you like about it? What <u>do</u> you like about it? These are questions which, once answered, will eventually lead to your product. They are also additional tools for sorting out barriers.

You look at the end product then figure out the why, where, when and how to get it.

Having your end point (product) well known, even in wide open downhill sweepers, creates confidence and also sets you up correctly for what's ahead.

Product

End To Beginning

Work from the end back to the beginning of the turn to establish an ideal product. Know in advance, before going into the turn, where the exit should be. In other words, a rider must be able to "see" the product of the turn as he enters it. This enables him to keep the pieces and parts of the turn working toward that product and allows him to flow the parts together.

You can become hopelessly lost by continuing to "look" at a turn from beginning to end instead of from the end back to the beginning. Once you know where you're going, you can spend your attention more wisely on the problems that come up in the turn, such as traction, lean angle and passing. You'll have plenty of spare change left to handle them. Otherwise, without a product and destination, any rider will always find his or herself spending too much attention on what might happen at the end of a turn. Keeping your product in mind helps handle the uncertainty. This isn't always easy.

Product Adjustment

A **product** may change every lap because of factors like other rider's positions, changing wind or weather conditions, ruts in dirt and the body's physical power potential. Once there is a **product** established, whether or not it is perfect, it can be used as a yardstick to measure progress. Any changes made in the turn will change the product somewhat, but you'd be able to tell whether or not those changes are working.

As speed is increased through a turn, the product will change slightly—or perhaps a lot if the rider is a beginner. An experienced rider may make a change that is three feet from his previous **product** and one mph faster. A beginner's may change ten feet, and may be five mph faster during the course of the race or training session. A product gives something to shoot for—something to change. If you blow a turn, you can always go back to something less aggressive.

At first I was thinking too much. Now I get the general layout of the course and then begin prioritizing the gearing, braking and bike set up. I get to the speed last.

Locate the Product

Where and how you enter a turn is totally decided by what and where the product is. Going into a turn the way it looks from the approach doesn't always work out well in the end. For example, riders commonly begin the turn too early, greatly affecting their exit product. Any rider who lets his adrenaline make his decisions has not yet realized that: **A product is made in stages, one step at a time.** These stages of its development are marked by the sub-products as listed above.

Medium speed and slower speed turns will produce more **sub-products** than faster turns or sections. Riders don't have the time to make a lot of changes in faster turns; they must be kept as simple as possible to leave enough attention to do it right. Fast turns usually do not have multiple camber changes or elevation changes such as crests—if they did they wouldn't be fast turns. Velodromes, having no obstacles, offer the best examples of fast turns.

With short practice you have to accelerate this process of prioritizing your focus of attention.

Slow and medium speed turns often do have these kinds of changes, and may require dramatic steering adjustments, e.g., bermed turns in the dirt or straightening the bike just before a crest. To reach the desired product, these changes must be made at precise places on the road or trail. Any place that requires a change in order to reach a final product for that turn is definitely a sub-product.

Further Application

This idea can be expanded into other areas as well; an attack for example. Think of all the aspects one might consider when making an attack: terrain, one's own physical condition, length of event, others' physical conditions and so on. Only rarely does an all-out effort alone make for a successful assault on the competition; correctly weighing all of the aspects of an attack to gain your product separates victory from tenth place. **Products and sub-products are a source of information and a gauge of your progress and resources.**

Gearing, seat height, bar choice, clothing, how much and what food to eat, conditioning, practice and workout regimens; practically anything can be thought out clearly by identifying its products and sub-products, even your career as a whole.

Old Racer's Tale

Another important point is the **false idea** that riders must use up all of the road or track at the end of a turn, whether they have to or not. Perhaps this comes from the old "straightest line" cornering theory that says to begin the turn wide and exit it as wide as possible. Wherever it comes from, it not only isn't always true, but it can actually prevent you from going faster through the turns. How?

Letting the bike go wide at the exit just because there is road or trail left over can give **a false impression you're going as fast as you can**. You can fool yourself into believing it can't be done faster.

While figuring out the turns and dialing in the product, riders naturally use the information they've stored up from the last pass through that section or turn to decide if any changes can be made.

If the information says the bike went all the way to the edge of the course the last time through, it makes it difficult to decide to go faster this time. You know you'll go even wider if you go faster.

Hold That Line

The remedy for this common error is to hold the tightest line possible on the exit to get an accurate idea of <u>where</u> that speed takes your bike. By holding a tight line at the end of a turn and finding there are still eight feet of road left, you could reasonably assume it can be done faster, or you could pick the bike up and pedal sooner.

If the next time through there everything was kept the same, but only the speed was increased, and there are still five feet of road left, you can go faster yet. The whole point is, don't fool yourself by using up the road or trail when it isn't necessary. By handling the exits of most turns in this way, you'll begin to establish a very accurate product and good sub-products. This is engineering the turn to fit your riding style and increase confidence.

Deciding on a product, then making adjustments to improve upon it, puts a rider in control. He is not being taken in by the course, making useless changes just because there's an opportunity to do so.

Here again, the classic example is being sucked in[12] on the entrance of a decreasing radius turn. Riders go in fast because they can, then have to play some serious catch-up at the point it begins to tighten. Holding the speed down on the entrance offers the most possibilities for conquering it. That's you thinking now, not baiting yourself into making an error.

Cornerocide

Running low, inside lines on turn entries has obvious advantages for pass protection but should always be balanced out against what it will cost at the turn's exit (product).

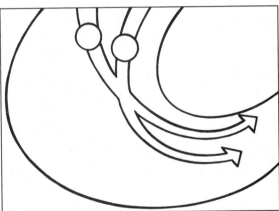

By taking low lines into turns riders actually create decreasing radius situations. They have to lean it more at mid-corner.

Your Results

The **products** and **sub-products** define a destination and accurately mark the places where you can make changes on the road, track or trail. They are the way of breaking down this process into smaller parts that can be understood and changed. Your confidence and smoothness increase **when you know where you're going and what to do when you get there**. The basic requirement as a rider is to observe where your products and sub-products are, what to do at those points and to remember them.

---

12 Tricked or deceived.

CHAPTER FOUR

What You See

Programming Your Computer Through the Eyes

What you see through the amber-colored lens of your Oakleys has much to do with how well you ride. The more you look, the more you see. You can't count the number of objects at any one spot on the course any more than you can count what you see just staring at the back of your hand. You can stop at any turn and look for hours at what's there to be seen. But while you're racing or riding down the road or trail, you can't stop to gaze.

Visual information rules. A rider's attention usually follows his line of vision.

How do you decide what to look at, what is important and what is not? And how do you use what you see? How can what you see help or hinder your riding? This chapter is about improving your riding by seeing correctly.

Where Are You?

The reason you look at points on the course is to learn where you are and where you are going. On any piece of road or trail a rider must look ahead to obtain information about where he is so he can decide what to do. You may have heard the expression "You go where you look." What this old <u>saw</u>[13] doesn't tell you is that you <u>can</u> go where you don't look, but you may have to use the brakes more than you want to. A cleaner, more in-control way of stating this is to say "Look where you want to go."

Reference Points

A **reference point** is a spot, area or object with a known location which clearly marks (identifies) a place. Reference points help riders know where they are on the course.

Two **reference points** present a better picture of your location. Three or more give you your exact location. Example: you're looking for a store on Main Street. You go to Main Street—that's one reference point. You find the right block—that's two. You check the numbers to see which direction they run—that's three. You decide which side of the street the store is on—that's four. You follow the numbers until you reach the store. That's five or more **reference points** that you would use in finding an address. On a race course or trail, before up or downhill sections, before turns or anywhere you need information, you do the same thing.

In training, you get all of the RPs so when you race they cost less attention.

Reference points are reminders of where you are. They are the basic building blocks for any plan.

I find RPs on every course, on most of the turns.

---

13 A maxim or proverb.

Familiar reference points allow you to look "around" the turn, well ahead of yourself, and with confidence.

You KNOW you are tired when you quit using RPs.

If you don't have enough reference points to know where you are, you're lost! *Is this familiar?*

Things happen fast on a bicycle moving at high speed and the situation changes constantly. The exact location on the road, trail or velodrome is very important because it determines the exact control actions needed. **If you don't know where you are, you also don't know what you're supposed to be doing.** Your location on a race course or road can be plotted in inches and feet—not in city blocks. It's up to you to decide what reference points to use and what to do when you reach them.

What to Use as Reference Points

Reference point types will vary from the velodrome to the road or trail, but the principle remains the same: **The best reference points (RPs) are something either on the course or very close to it.** On the road, a patch of asphalt, a painted line, a spot, a crack or curbing can be used. On the velodrome, there are advertising signs, measurement markers and light poles. On the trail, distinguishable trees and rocks work well. Whatever the venue, the basic rule is **anything that doesn't move can be a reference point**.

One Foot In

The RPs chosen should be **in your line of vision and along your path of travel**. Objects too far from the actual riding surface will take attention away from the course or trail. RPs must be easy to find to be usable. At times riders use the edge of the road or trail, **but a point that's a foot in from the edge is better** because it keeps the attention on course. In all cases, going to the limit with an exit RP that's one foot from the edge, **there would still be a foot left over**.

The RPs (dirt, ruts, berm, rock) are actually signs telling the rider what to do, like "brake," "pedal," "sit up," "full power," "turn," "slide," "lean." A reference point gives you information. It signals both <u>where</u> and <u>how much</u> you should be doing.

Speak To Me

A reference point is not only something that can easily be seen on or near the course; **it must mean something to you when you see it**. Every time it's passed or approached, this point must communicate a message, like "This is where I begin looking for my turn marker," or "If I'm to the right of this too much I'll hit a bump, but to the left of it I'm all right" or, "This is where I begin my turn." **Reference points are economical reminders of where you are or what action you must take; they save attention.**

Choosing something as a reference point just because it's there and easy to see may not be profitable; it might not be the right RP because it's too far off line or it doesn't work for the speed you're traveling; but generally speaking, RPs that are directly in the line of travel establish a positive location on the course lengthwise. RPs along the side establish a positive location in relation to the width of the course. And of course, fixing attention on any RP for too long will result in losing some perspective on the course. The bottom line for an RP is does it <u>work</u>?

Now, I'm always setting points for brake on and off, front and rear, downshifting and where to jump.

RP Decisions

On any riding surface, attention can hang up on most any-thing. Chewed up or discolored pavement and changing scenery off-road are classic attention stickers but rarely affect the way the bike actually handles. In traffic, any car (parked or in motion), pedestrian, surface irregularity, traffic light, intersection, anything there is, can claim cash from that precious $10 worth of attention. So why do we look at them? What if we didn't look at them? When a rider becomes aware of fixed attention, he knows it detracts from his riding. The solution is simple: find out which ones are usable reference points and **abandon all unnecessary ones**. It's a positive action towards freeing up attention and gaining perspective.

Everything you notice costs attention. Each type of riding has a different budget.

I assign more RPs in sections that are difficult for me—they are my guide, like following a recipe.

How to Use A Reference Point

Two or more reference points are needed to accurately locate yourself on the course. Narrowing attention to only one object sets people up to become a victim of <u>target fixation</u> where they go to that RP because they don't have anything else to do. This occurs in a panic situation and can happen anywhere on a course, road or

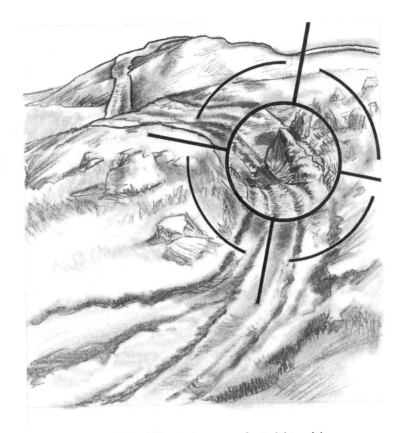

*Having too few
reference points
causes target fixation.*

trail. If there are enough familiar RPs to be comfortable with any
area or space, then target fixation is less likely to occur.

    When there are sufficient RPs in any turn or section of a race
course, the scene moving in front of the rider appears to move
smoothly, like a wide-screen, 70mm movie. Too few and the scene
looks like an old-time movie, bouncing and jerking along. Having
only one RP is like watching a single frame from a slide show—nice
picture, but where do you go from there?

    No doubt you've heard that you must look down the road to
where you're going, not where you are. This is good information—

*This is really important for
downhills.*

*Having enough
reference points
"opens up" the course,
making it appear larger,
and costs less of your
attention.*

you need those additional RPs to locate yourself on the course. Looking too close to the bicycle won't help you find it.

High Speed Reference Points

At twenty mph a bike is traveling at thirty feet per second; at thirty mph, forty four feet per second and at fifty mph plus on those descents, a bike is hurtling through space at seventy-five feet per second. That second ticks by very quickly, and if you're not ready for the next move, ahead of time, you'll make a mistake. **Looking ahead for reference points creates time** to prepare for the next move so there are fewer surprises and everything goes smoothly.

This idea can be taken too far, however. I've seen riders looking way too far ahead while rounding a tight hairpin turn. They were ignoring what was to be seen in front of them, like curbing and pot-holes. Still, other riders in the same turn were looking at the curbing and holes, but not until they were right on top of them. Both of these extremes are unworkable; they produce uncertain riding through the turn. If you need to look far down the road to see where the breakaway group is, do so in the straight-aways—where the operations of riding are less crucial. Using good RPs is a skill which is taught and the mark of an accomplished rider.

Where to Look

Two factors will help determine where to look while riding or racing.

1. At speed, the further ahead anyone looks, the slower they believe they're going; the closer they look, the faster they believe they're going. Look far enough ahead to avoid accelerating the scene but not so far that you lose your feel for where you are on the course. With RPs, there is a choice of where to look.

2. Having enough RPs has the effect of <u>opening up</u> the course, making it appear larger. Looking too far ahead or too close to the bike, the course seems to narrow. If this begins happening, it is a signal to either change RPs or to find more of them in that turn or section of the course.

These are guidelines. Adjust RPs so the scene is moving at the right speed, and so you can see enough to keep the course "opened up."

Having only one RP is like having only one bicycle. If it breaks, you stay home. If you have another bicycle, you can easily use the one that works. With only one reference point, or bike, it becomes too valuable and necessary. If you find your attention is fixed on one point of the road or trail, it's because you don't have another ready to use. **That one becomes overly valuable and riders tend to then overuse it.** You'll depend upon it for too much information and might begin staring at it. It's easy to become slightly lost when it no longer accurately marks where you are or what to do. If you find your attention becoming fixed on one RP, you need to find another in the area so the "movie" will smooth out.

When you really know the course it flows. When you aren't familiar with it you are tense.

Looking out of a turn relaxes me. Looking ahead makes you feel like the turn is already over.

RPs too close is like night riding with a light 8 ft. in front of you—everything feels fast.

When I get nervous I'll target fix and hit something.

Stepping Stones

Reference points are stepping stones to the products and sub-products in a turn or a series of turns. These little steps lead to the major changes necessary to get yourself and your bicycle around the turns faster and with more confidence. RPs signal the points on the course where those changes will be made.

Sometimes I become obsessed with a section and run it 5 times until I get my RPs and understand it.

Concentration

On the road, track or trail, concentration is a smooth flow or chain of events that moves along without a break. Reference points are part of that chain, one link depending on the next for strength and a continuous flow. If one link breaks, the entire chain stays broken until it can be repaired or replaced. If there is a section of the course with no or too few RPs, that chain of concentration will be stressed and will break. **Reference points are the building blocks of concentration.**

Concentration has something to do with reference points. Too few or too many won't work.

Unconcentrate

Let's get back to the idea of attention and how much of it a rider has; that $10 dollar bill. When concentration is good, just enough of it is spent on each RP so that where you are and what to do are clear. This keeps that steady flow going. When there are too few RPs in an area, most of that attention will be spent in trying to fix this bad situation. **The points or places on the course that you do not know or understand will occupy most of your attention.**

Having enough RPs allows for a correct budget of attention to be spent on each one and to get the information you need. That provides enough left over to buy other things, to make small changes in riding that will help you to go faster and aid power conservation and recovery needs as well. **Everything you do on**

Sleep is out of the question the night before a race if I don't have a section of the course MEMORIZED.

the course takes up some attention. When there aren't enough RPs, attention goes right to that area and can—or will—break the concentration.

Some of the strangest things happen when there is a break in concentration. According to one rider, every time his concentration broke he began thinking of a leaking faucet at home. Your mind may not wander to a leaking faucet but when concentration breaks, other things come into the mind, making the rider more of a passenger than a pilot.

Concentration—The Twist

There's a twist to this subject of concentration; when it's there, it doesn't seem you're looking at anything in particular. The reference points just blend into the scene in front. When asked, "What do you look at in the turns?" top riders often say, "I don't really look at anything." But is this really what they mean?

When concentration is good, we just spend nickels and dimes on the RPs and none of them captures too much attention. An example of this is that one of the major differences between riders is their ability to learn new courses. Learning a course means **knowing where you are on the course.** Some riders can do it right away, others can never do it. Both guys have to learn where they are by reference points; the top riders just do it so fast they can beat others on their favorite road or trail the second time they see it! So much for the home field advantage. One factor that separates the top riders from the rest of the field is that they pick up RPs quickly and accurately to a point where they can see the whole scene without having to pick out the individual RPs.

Enough Reference Points

Once someone has enough RPs, he can see the whole scene comfortably without having to stare at the RPs individually. This is a real goal, and the individual building blocks of that scene are the RPs. If concentration becomes lost you'd have to go back and rely on or relocate yourself with the RPs that are familiar. That's how to restore concentration immediately: **Go back to the reference points you know and pick up the thread of concentration.** If there aren't enough RPs in that area, it'll cost time in the race as you hesitate and tighten up or even hit the brakes.

Do Not Read Past This Next Paragraph Until You Have Completed the Experiment

1. Get a stopwatch.
2. Sit down in a comfortable chair.
3. Close your eyes and think of a race course you're familiar with. Start the watch and run through a complete lap on the course or a complete downhill run. Do it from memory. Try to go through it as fast as you did the last time you rode it. You are timing your memory of the course and how you rode it.
4. Now, try it again.

With using RPs I can get to race pace much quicker.

I used to think going over a section many times would just make it "sink in" but finding RPs shortcuts that.

If I can't draw it I don't know it. I test myself to see if it's clear in my mind.

Find a stopwatch or a wall clock with a second hand and try this eye-opening experiment. Do it again after you've ridden the course.

Memory Lap

If you're like most riders, the course or lap time recall will be either much too long or much too short. If you just broke the down-hill course record or the absolute lap record by twenty or thirty seconds, or if you added twenty or thirty seconds to your best times, it means the same thing—not enough <u>usable</u> reference points.

The slow-time rider's "movie" is incomplete and he finds himself stargazing at the places where he has no RPs. His attention is on the areas of the course he does not know.

In the very fast-time situation, the rider still hasn't got enough RPs so he flits from one to the next very quickly because those are what he does know. The RPs may be poor choices as well, like billboards, lakes and other landmarks too far off course. **Having sufficient and quality RPs gives you a better sense of time because you now have points to mark your motion around the course or down the trail.** Attention goes either to the places you know very well, or to the place you don't know very well. Or it becomes split between the two. This costs a lot of attention and it then can't be spent on other things.

Too many RPs is a frantic attempt by the rider to make sense out of the scenes he looks at but in the end it is the same thing: too few usable RPs.

I get RPs first, then sections with RPs, and then whole sections come together. But RPs are the building blocks.

Find the Lost RPs

Here's an easy method you can use to discover where you don't have enough RPs.

1. Close your eyes.
2. Carefully run through your own mental "movie" of the course or trail as if you were riding.

3. "Ride" through one complete lap or a previously timed section in your memory.
4. Open your eyes and draw each turn on a separate sheet of paper, marking the reference points you're sure of in each turn.
5. Make a note of what each means to you, like: braking point, steering change, location on the course, bump, acceleration point, exit marker, product, ruts coming up, shift point, attack section, etc.
6. Close your eyes again and go back over your "movie," noticing the places you hesitate or go blank, where the scene gets foggy or when you hurry through it too fast. Each of these situations indicates you have too few reference points at these locations.
7. Now make a note on your turn drawings at each place you have a blank spot or any other problem from step 6 above.
8. Find either more RPs or more accurate ones for those areas the next time you ride that course or trail.
9. Eliminate unnecessary RPs.

Good RPs help you keep a steady flow of concentration. You spend (use) RPs to save attention.

In Spain my second year I crashed 5 or 6 times from not knowing the course and not knowing how to know it.

This method can be used to help find both weak and strong spots. Riders use their memory of turns for this drill and they rely on that when they ride. Knowing where to go is a big part of the thread of concentration. One valuable visual goal would be to see the whole scene in front without having to spend a lot of attention on any one point. You'd be building that scene with individual reference points.

Concentration And RPs

The trick to using RPs and gaining concentration is that we have to look at something. Eyes work by focusing on some object or some plane, then everything in that plane is in focus, like on a movie screen. The eyes may be looking at only one area of the screen, but the entire screen is in focus.

Another point is that when eyes move, they do so in short stopping movements. They flit from one object to another like a butterfly. If you try to sweep the eyes across a scene without stopping on anything, the scene becomes a blur. Try it.

A rider's problem is that he wants to see the course or trail in front of him flowing as a whole scene, to maintain a steady flow of concentration, but his eyes don't work that way. If he stares at one reference point too long, he'll experience a form of tunnel vision. But because of the way his eyes work, he has to look at some specific thing! There's the twist.

See Fast

How do the top riders manage to ride so fast and see all they need to without experiencing problems in seeing? Here's a drill that will help you practice the proper seeing techniques.

1. Find a wall that is entirely visible to you, where you can see all four corners by moving your eyes but not your head.
2. Focus your eyes on a spot in the middle of the wall.
3. Remain focused on that spot, then move your attention, <u>not</u> your eyes, to the upper right-hand corner of the wall.
4. Still focusing on that spot, move your attention to different places on the wall. You are looking at one spot but are aware of the other areas of the wall.
5. Still focusing on that spot, move your attention to the objects between you and the wall, and on the wall as well.

Having RPs directly affects my lap times and consistency.

Collecting visual information costs time and attention.

The Whole Picture

Anyone can see the whole scene while still looking at one place or spot! You probably noticed that you wanted to move your eyes from the spot you were focused on to the spot to which your attention had gone. This drill becomes easier with practice. Practice moving your attention around while looking at one spot or area as you're driving to the races or just sitting in a chair. It's a skill that may take time to develop if you haven't mastered it already.

Now, when you see the whole scene in this way you have to realize that the points in the scene must be well known to you. You need the reference points in the scene to make the scene. If you don't know the RPs your eyes will <u>hunt</u> for something that is familiar and lose the whole-scene effect.

Being able to see the course in front as a whole scene makes riding much easier and brings concentration back if it falters. As can be seen in the drill above, it is where attention is directed, where the ten dollar bill is spent, that's much more important than what is being looked at. Attention must be spent economically, and looking at the whole scene rather than at one thing is spending it very wisely, and getting back interest on the investment. It may require practice. *Can you do it?*

I've been making drawings of each track in detail and now I see other riders doing it too.

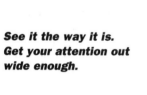

See it the way it is. Get your attention out wide enough.

You want to look down the course but also be aware of where you are now.

Loss Of Concentration

When we see how well it works to look at the whole scene as a tool for increasing concentration, it seems odd that concentration normally means to focus down on something. That's exactly what we don't want! Here is another drill.

1. Pick six spots in front of you that you feel would be in your normal field of vision, as if you were looking at the road and had six RPs.
2. Move your eyes as rapidly as possible from one to the

next, stopping as briefly as possible to focus on each before moving to the next.

3. Do this for about thirty seconds.
4. How do you feel?

Almost everyone gets at least some slight feeling of disorientation if not mild dizziness from doing this. Disorientation is the primary cause of mental fatigue while riding a bicycle, especially when you're riding fast.

Another drill:

1. Pick the same six spots as above.
2. This time, while moving your eyes from one to the other, keep your field of attention wide so you are aware of the whole area, while shifting your focus from one point to the other.
3. Is that easier on you?
4. Finally, just to make you feel better, stare at your farthest point and shift your awareness, not your eyes, from each one of the six points to the next.
5. Better? It should be.

Controlled View

The ability to get this whole-scene or wide-screen view is clearly under your control **when you remember to do it**. Looking around the room now, it is practically impossible to see it any other way but wide. As you ride faster your view can narrow but it doesn't have to.

On a good day my attention is wide and I feel like my vision is fluid but focused at the same time.

Mechanically speaking, the eye doesn't actually shut down its peripheral input when it fixes on objects; you simply aren't aware of the whole scene when your attention is captured or directed elsewhere. When you remember to do it, **the width of your awareness is totally controlled by the mind**. Can you train yourself to remember? Will practice help put you more in control than you are now? Decide for yourself. Is your attention wide right now? Could it be "held out" that wide on demand? *Will you practice?*

Wide View is like relaxing your brain. I try to achieve that state where you don't have to fixate.

Too Wide, Too long

On a bicycle, setting both short and long targets for pedaling can help. Putting attention too wide or too far ahead can make the short-term goals seem too long and the speed seem too slow. Dividing a hill into several visual sections, where you stand up for one and sit for the other, or simply noting mile or kilo markers, can give a sense of accomplishing the tasks and a gauge for strength reserves as well.

When I'm not riding well my attention is too focused and my field of view is always microscopic.

There is an endless variety of visual games riders play with themselves, e.g., looking close to the bike then up ahead every now and then to see how much distance has been covered, not looking at the distance covered and so on. Every rider plays these visual games in some fashion or another. Make up your own games.

WHAT YOU SEE <u>IS</u> WHAT YOU GET.

CHAPTER FIVE

Timing

Putting Things In Order

Timing really has nothing to do with a rider's sense of clock time. It has to do with **taking the correct action at exactly the correct place**. The whole idea of timing is to assemble reference points, products and sub-products so they're useful on the course. Doing the right thing at the wrong place produces very poor results, as does knowing what to do, but not exactly where to do it.

A Timing Lesson

The piano, that is where I learned timing. The pause between notes is as important as the note.

I learned my life timing lesson on skateboards and David learned his from mastering deep powder snow skiing. This is how his went:

"I could turn all right on firm snow but when my skis sank below the surface in the soft stuff, I was in trouble and would fall. At first I worked on various techniques to handle the problem. I had been 'swiveling' the skis underfoot to turn and it didn't work. So I switched to a carving-on-the-edges technique for the powder, but that was even worse. Finally, I discovered that I simply had too much weight on the skis for any technique to work.

Timing is doing. The correct action at the exact right place opens the door to improvement.

"Unweighting your body's mass from the skis for a split second allows you to change edges and initiate the turn, then the even weight distribution allows you to complete the turn on that edge. The proper way to turn was a combination of technique and **timing**: an even weight distribution over the

length of the ski plus a perfectly timed 'unweighting' motion. "Once I got it right, skiing on any type of snow and terrain became much easier. Once the **timing** was understood, I was ready to improve."

Slowing Down For The Turns

A solid lesson like that one is great when the basic is captured, applied to other activities and found to work there as well. Many of the most obvious mistakes made by riders aren't based on their style but are simply timing errors. They do the right stuff but at the wrong time. Take braking for example.

In turns where the brakes are used, **exactly where they're let off and when the steering is begun** can make a great difference in the execution of that maneuver. Such a change can be made in many different ways, but timing is the key that unlocks the mystery of smooth, fast and in-control turn entries. Let's look at all the possibilities:

1. You can finish the braking, then turn/lean and coast.
2. You can finish the braking while beginning to turn/lean, then coast.
3. You can finish the braking, then turn/lean and start pedaling.
4. You can finish the braking, then pedal up to your turning speed and take the turn.
5. You can finish the braking after starting to turn/lean, then pedal.
6. You can finish the braking after you've turned/leaned completely, then pedal.

In riding, the pause or the timing of when to dive into the turn is just as important.

You can play all the notes of a song but without the timing it would be unrecognizable.

This makes you think of all the possibilities and makes you think of preparing your timing for the turn.

Your body position, braking and acceleration all affect weight transfer to the front or rear wheel. Correctly timing these weight shifts for the conditions is a critical part of riding.

What Happens

In 1. above, most of the weight shifts to the front wheel of the bike—under normal braking. As much as 75% to the front; more if you brake harder. When the brakes are released, the weight balances out to more of a 50/50 distribution. When the rider dives into the turn, the cornering forces put the weight onto the front end again right as the turn is entered, with the rear end light. Finally, as the bike settles into the turn, the load evens up somewhat, but it's still heavy up front from deceleration. These weight shift changes affect the steering and reduce stability and traction.

Going through those six turn-entry scenarios based on this data you can come up with what your bike will do weight-wise in each. On a bike with suspension, these weight shifts are more obvious because the bike's geometry[14] changes, but they affect rigid framed machines in the same way.

The basics are simple enough:
- Brakes-on equals lots of weight forward.
- Power-on equals weight rearward.
- The front wheel **sees** the cornering load first.
- Coasting in the turn equals some weight forward plus the overall increase in weight on both wheels from the cornering forces.

Timing VS Handling

If the wheel loads on any vehicle were always the same (even), cornering would be much simpler. To get into a turn smoothly and correctly, the braking and turning must be timed correctly so that weight distribution stays as steady as possible at the point the brakes are let off and the turn is entered. Weight shifting back and forth makes the bike unpredictable, especially when it comes to traction.

If their **timing** is off, riders may complain that the bike handles poorly, thinking it could be the frame geometry, the tires or any number of mechanical things. Any of these things could be true, but don't buy a new bike until the most common cause of poor handling is eliminated—the rider's **timing** of steering, braking and body weight/position distribution.

Your Timing Targets

Let's state that again: the target, or sub-product for any turn in which you brake and turn in succession is **timing the braking, body position, steering and pedaling so that weight distribution is kept as consistent as possible**.

In fast S and compound turns, when two or more turns are strung together and cannot be taken flat out, timing is important. The faster they're ridden, the stiffer the steering becomes. On a quick right/left or left/right combination, time the steering changes so you are generating the least downward force on the bars just before the transition from side to side. This lightens the front end

My music teacher thought poor timing was a disaster, it definitely is with bicycle riding.

Just knowing this information adds something to riding. Otherwise you feel things and don't know why.

After reading this I became more aware of what could be done and it made my turns smoother.

---

14 The up or down angle of the bike compared to its at-rest position.

and weights the rear wheel, making the steering easier, and lessens the front tires tendency to slide. In soft, high traction dirt and at slower speeds, it is exactly the opposite. You'll want the front to bite and the weight helps. When done correctly for either situation, even a bike with poor or outdated geometry will handle just fine. When done wrong, the best bike in the world will handle poorly, especially on rough surfaces.

Back Off Time

Braking between turns should be avoided when possible because riders tend to overuse brakes. Pedaling hard then backing off for a second, then steering, then a few more pedal strokes in between two connected turns can actually get a rider through quicker than going in super fast and having to use the brakes. A better timed and overall smoother approach to S-turns doesn't seem as dramatic but is usually faster. Avoid the on and offs of snapping at the brakes and pedals. Spot-on timing is the basis of smooth speed.

Tiredness = Loss of Timing

When you become tired, the first thing you lose is your timing. Loss of timing generally brings about a mild panic situation where the rider notices he is late turning or getting back in the pedals, and so on, then tries to make up the difference with gobs of effort. Big mistake, it only gets worse. This is a major reason why it's important to have reference points and products well established; even when tired there is still something to shoot for.

Points of Timing

Sub-products, the major steps or changes in a turn, could also be called **points of timing** (POT).

Points of timing are places on the course where you do something: brake, stop braking, pedal, shift, stand up, sit down, turn, slide, back off, shift weight, position for a jump. There is always an action connected to such a point. Knowing **where** the POTs are and **what** to do at each, means you won't have to slow down as much when you become tired, at least in the turns. More speed may not be an option, but the competition is probably suffering timing problems too. Just being able to maintain, with no additional effort required, is an edge.

One more point on this—not all RPs are points of timing. Some only indicate where you are, signaling an important upcoming change like shifting, braking, out of the saddle, and so on.

Pack Timing

How does this relate to pack riding where timing largely depends on other riders? Pack riding is timing the riding actions with those around you and there are two views of it. In one, you'd do what everyone else does. In the second, you'd predict and control what will happen.

Strategically speaking, someone is in control of any pack; setting the pace, the line, the attitude of the race and it might as

The faster you go the earlier you want to get set to turn the bike.

You do not want to brake in esses.

Pumping the bike in turns gets it to hook up and turn better, like pumping on a swing.

Pumping works in loose stuff too but you are aware it will get loose on the upstroke.

POTs are different than RPs; they are a place where you do something.

well be you—when and if you choose. **The rider who is in control of the timing is in control of the pack**.

Timing and the Road You Ride

This is another way to understand what a bike does in a turn.

Changes in the road or trail affect timing dramatically. You not only have to work the brakes, gears and pedals correctly, you also have to fit these into the camber and radius changes. For instance, if a rider were coming up to a banked turn where he'd have to use the brakes first, he should know that this type of turn will create more downward pressure on the bike than would a similar turn that is flat with no banking.

To go in perfectly, you'd let off the brakes right where the banking starts, just as the tires and wheels are beginning to take the cornering loads. This produces the smoothest entry. **Back off of the brakes just as the turn takes over the job of compressing you and your bike**. Braking too hard reduces the cornering speed and the bike will "straighten" up when it hits the banking or berm, and will run wide as it unloads the wheels. Not using enough brake or letting them off too soon, then hitting the banking, causes the cornering force load to the tires and wheels to be abrupt. Banks and berms require good control of timing.

In off-camber turns:
1. Spend as little time in them as possible.
2. Design your plan around the forces pulling you to the outside of the turn.

Off-Camber Timing

In an off-camber section it is better to have yourself and the bike light, which means as vertical as possible to keep from excessively drifting to the outside. **Timing** the control operations for a constant speed as well as a stable body position/weight distribution is critical in off-camber situations because traction deteriorates more rapidly.

Any braking will always load the front wheel and could cause the front-end to slide out. This, of course, is most apparent in off-camber dirt sections.

Braking in turns just makes the bike go straight to the outside.

The rider might be puzzled; whereas braking usually helps him get through turns when he's going too fast, here he braked and still crashed. The point is that weight changes and control actions are all amplified in an off-camber situation and losing front wheel traction is the usual unwanted result. In an off camber section, **POTs** are set so the bike is slowing the least amount possible in the most off-camber portion in order to prevent too much weight transfer.

Changing the Course with Timing

In a section of the course where a dip weights you and the bike fully it is sometimes possible to counteract the compression by timing body weight shifts for just that point. A swift rearward weight shift while pulling back on the handlebars just before the dip, or a "bunny-hop" type upward movement right at the dip may stop some of the swerving and bobbing that occurs from the compression.

Standing on the pedals and using your legs as suspension will also produce added stability. This action depends completely on timing. In fact, it is the solution to practically every rough terrain situation there is.

Timing can change the course conditions for better or worse. Get the **POTs** right and it can work. If you don't, it won't.

Conditions do change but having your plan set gives you a real place to start.

Products and Timing

The real goal is still the overall **product** for any turn. In the corners, you'd still want the maximum speed, undisturbed momentum throughout and an exit setup for the best straight-away speed to get into the next turn.

All the RPs, POTs and sub-products must make the product better or you have done a lot of fancy riding that is slow riding. Sometimes it's a better handling to go directly through a rough section of the course a little skittery and chirping the rear wheel than to figure a smoother but slower way around it. Your measure of progress is in whether or not the **product** is improving.

On downhill you sometimes have to change your braking points because the surface gets rippled.

Timing in Perspective

To put **timing** in perspective, let's take a look at two types of turns; first a basic velodrome maneuver to demonstrate timing, then a complicated road turn.

Up On the Banking

Let's say the rider is moving down the straight-away at high speed low on the track and wishes to run at the top of the banking. When he reaches the turn he cuts off the power and goes "straight" up the banking. As he's climbing, his speed slows quickly and the G-force of "hitting the wall" of banking will begin to lessen.

At some point at the top of the ascent, the bike will become virtually weightless for a moment and if the rider has **timed** it right, this will be at the exact spot where he wished to make his steering change for the tactics he has in mind: flatten out and ride a high line or turn back down the banking. **Timing** is the key to a smooth and energy efficient steering maneuver.

Turn Hell

Let's create a turn with a temperamental personality. First, let's create a slightly downhill S-turn leading to a flat decreasing-radius turn at the bottom. The S allows the rider to power on until it's time to enter the DR turn at the bottom. This DR turn is deceptive. It's banked going in, then flattens out in the middle, banks again and finally flattens out for the exit.

Leaving the S at full speed, most riders will brake before entering the DR turn at the bottom, creating an unwanted, destabilizing weight shift to the front end just as the banking is entered. Typically, riders overuse the brakes, then, once they feel the security of the banking, must "catch up"—accelerate through the

I set POTs that say "Relax, get your head together."

Pull it together. Once you figure out the surface changes, what you actually did to go well or poorly, what product you are trying to achieve and your RPs, timing becomes the key to making it all work together.

wide, banked turn entry. The combination of releasing the brake and powering on through this first banked section transfers weight to the rear wheel, which is fine—for about two pedal strokes.

But now, entering the flat center section means an abrupt cut in power for pedal clearance and an imperative lean angle increase to hold the line. The steeper lean angle offers less traction, and combined with the weight transfer, the front end now has a precarious feeling. Some riders will even tag the brake to counteract the outward bound corner force, amplifying the error.

The turn now begins to tighten, producing a mild panic where the brakes may again seem the only answer. But if the brakes are used as the rider enters the next banked section, this will slow him even more, and only adds load to the front end. This prompts him to try for a pedal stroke to compensate, but he's now reached the flat exit section where more lean is needed to stay on line, further delaying his acceleration out.

All of this busy work would look and feel pretty rough. That turn has four camber changes, two radius changes and an elevation change, but with some understanding and good timing, its mysteries can be unraveled and ridden.

Right Timing

There is absolutely nothing wrong with riders using start and stop pedaling techniques or even going on and off the brakes. The problem is where they are doing it. Timing is everything and the basics must be in place to make it work.

First, the **road's changes** must be identified. These are often difficult to spot while riding.

Second, **points of timing** are established to signal the changes. This is <u>vital</u>. At forty-four feet per second (30 mph), being off even a quarter second can start a chain of errors.

Third, an overall **product** is determined. This eliminates the frantic rush to handle all of the self-created errors, and establishes a plan in the process.

Fourth, a **plan** is established to take advantage of the banking. Use the rule of thumb: be low on the banking when leaving it.

My description of the rider going through this turn may sound like a nightmare, but watching novice racers go through it is worse. Their expressions, their death grips on the bars, the skidding, the cursing—there's always a big crowd around these types of turns to see the crashes.

For the rider, this can evolve into a problem of sorts after he's ridden it a few times in that he can begin to feel stupid because of his inability to control the bike. Most riders will compromise and try a constant-radius line, pretending it's all just one turn, with no real camber or radius changes!

Longer races leave more room for error. Short downhills must be sharp and precise.

Timing Solution

A fast plan in this turn would work with its changes.

1. Back off slightly through the downhill S and use the bank-

ing's resistance (going in) to slow the bike instead of the brakes.

2. Target the exit of the first banked section to be low to the inside. This creates more track as the bike begins to swing wide.

3. Don't fight the flat, middle section of the turn. Where it flattens out, let the bike drift out, then:

4. Use the banking on the exit to its best advantage, starting high and exiting low, getting the power on early.

This line is called the <u>low-high-low</u>. Low in, high middle and low out; which is a good handling for many double-apex turns, especially in the dirt. The **timing** must be correct for it to work. Turns with fewer changes can be equally baffling if the timing is wrong.

Some riders, of course, can go through this type of turn very fast by keeping up a fever pitch of concentration and catlike reflexes, but they won't be as fast or as consistent as someone who understands the turn. And riding at or past your concentration limit wears you out sooner.

Shaving the Course

You don't have to keep up a razor's edge of concentration everywhere on the course. You've still got that ten dollars worth of attention you're trying to spend wisely. Continuing to spend all of it all the time will use it up. In common speak this is called "stress." For example, spending the whole ten dollars to go down the straight is a waste. Relax. Put it in savings to draw interest, then withdraw it again for the next turn or for changes in the dynamics and strategy of the race.

Any rider's attention and ability to concentrate come and go. By spending attention only when necessary, it will be there when it's needed. This is another level of understanding timing—the recognition of where the precision work is essential, and where you can cool it when it's not.

It's easy to forget to breathe in BMX because the jumps take all your attention.

Race Pace

After long races riders sometimes say that they were pacing themselves, trying to relax, but they went faster than in the short races. Some situations force riders to get smart. Using this relaxed attitude in the shorter races can help a rider be sharp there as well. On the velodrome, for example, having riders do a 200 meter sprint at 90% effort often yields faster times than a flat-out, 100% effort!

Usually it is the result of something idiotically simple—the rider remembers to breathe. Riders often try to replace good timing with more effort and it is not a substitute. Just figure where your POTs are and what you're supposed to be doing at each one.

Attack Points

Set up a reference point to signal where to start paying attention or concentrating. For instance, attacks usually occur coming out of the corners and in the straights, not at the entry or in the middle of turns where everyone is concentrating on making it through. Create "attack" reference points for the places you think they're most likely to occur, use them for your own attack plans and to keep tabs on the competition as well. Get ready <u>when</u> you see the RP, not before.

In downhill you can't tell when to attack so you wind up attacking all he time.

Spend attention only when necessary. good points of timing tell you where to spend and where to save.

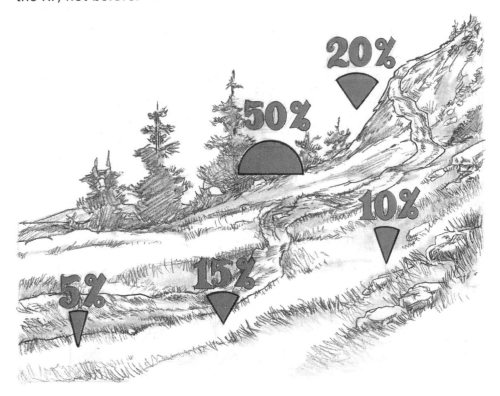

Relax

Top athletes in every sport have all eventually come to the realization that **to relax is to win**. For a novice rider who has yet to realize this, the whole concept seems absurd; he's convinced that "effort" is the answer. You'd have to be twenty-five percent stronger than you are now to replace the performance gains in store for you with good timing.

That riders have to transcend this "effort band" to realize this is normal, but I'd be safe in saying that no rider will reach the top without it. Once a good sense of timing comes into focus, effort will fall away like a bad dream and be replaced by confidence and an economy of motion you've only dreamed of. Amazingly enough, it totally depends on where you spend your **attention**, the one thing in riding and racing you have the most control over—when you remember to exercise it. Spending your attention wisely is the answer now and always will be.

Rhythm = Timing

Riders talk about the rhythm of a race course or road, of getting the flow of the trail. This is **timing**. The rider is fitting himself and his equipment into the course and all the actions he has to perform. The basis of timing is understanding. Fast reflexes are not a substitute.

Timing is both an idea and an action. It is knowing what to do and where to do it. Anyone can look back over his riding and recall situations which, because of poor timing, became uncomfortable. The second part is going out and actually doing it. **Get the timing right first—then add the speed**.

In cross-country I attack before a downhill because I know I'm going to drop that rider on the downhill section.

I made my attack a little too soon at the World's this year and had to settle for the silver.

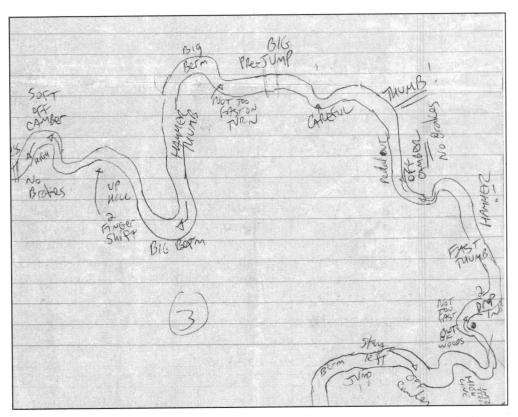

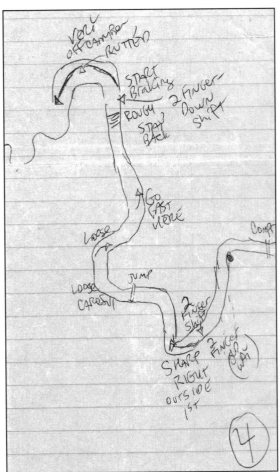

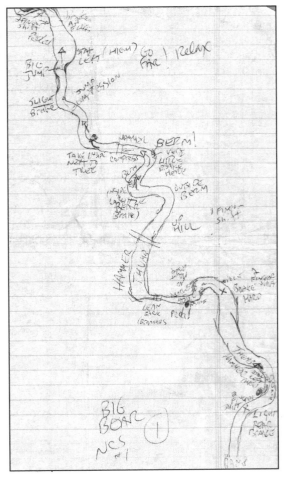

Samples of Marla's course drawings.

CHAPTER SIX

Decisions

Decision-Making: Recipe for Skill

Having a plan helps me be decisive.

Decisions make up the very fabric of life, and the alternative is a grim one—indecision. The act of racing is an intricately woven pattern of decisions, finely laced with drive, success, skill, technique and competition; all of it embroidered with enormous physical stress. Indeed, practically every movement and action is based upon a **decision**. Only **panic reactions**, deftly woven in by nature for raw survival purposes, are truly automatic, and many of them can be unraveled and overridden by the simple and efficient use of **decision**. More often than not, whole areas of activity can be cleared up just from the knowledge that a decision point has been reached <u>or should be made</u>. **Decisions define the stages of your improvement.**

Decisions in motion. A rider's "style" is the result of his decisions. Making decisions puts you in control.

Decisions save attention.

Garden Variety Decisions

Inspecting any riding function will uncover many potential and actual decisions. For example, riders often say gear changes become "automatic," but let's look closer at this common function of riding.

Dealing with terrain you have to be decisive.

- You **decide** when you're pedaling at the right RPM.
- You **decide** at what speed to make the shift.
- You **decide** where on the course to shift.
- You **decide** how much to back off the power or not.
- You **decide** how many gears to change, up or down.
- You **decide** which hand to use on older shifters.
- You **decide** how many fingers to use on the lever.
- You **decide** to be sitting or standing during the shift.
- You **decide** on a fore or aft body position.
- You **decide** on a larger gear for resting purposes.
- You **decide** on a specific gear for tactical reasons.
- You **decide** to fool or to distract the competition with a gear change.
- You **decide** on a smaller gear for loosening up the legs.

You may spend only a nickel or a dime of your **attention** on these **decisions**, but you are spending <u>something</u>. Recall how much attention you once spent on them compared to now? **Once you have made a <u>decision</u>, it costs less attention to perform the action.**

63

Decide

My decisions are made before the morning of the race, even for contingencies like rain.

Either operate by decisions or in panic mode; there really isn't any in between. Your **decisions** are based on:

1. Past actions that will now apply.
2. Accurate present time observations that open the door to removing barriers.
3. The ability to confidently predict what will be needed for the future.

It doesn't take <u>much</u> attention to decide whether to accelerate sitting in the saddle or standing up, but it takes some. On the flip side, the two most obvious things about panic are:

1. The person's inability to coolly observe and decide on the appropriate action to take.
2. Terror-stricken, often fixated eyes or being frozen at the controls are proof of #1.

How to Decide

Decisions are the details of your overall plan. Making a decision gives you a place to start and something to change, or stop if it doesn't work out.

Generally, a decision can be arrived at in one of two ways. One is to work at the problem until it's narrowed down by the process of elimination. This method is called **trial and error**

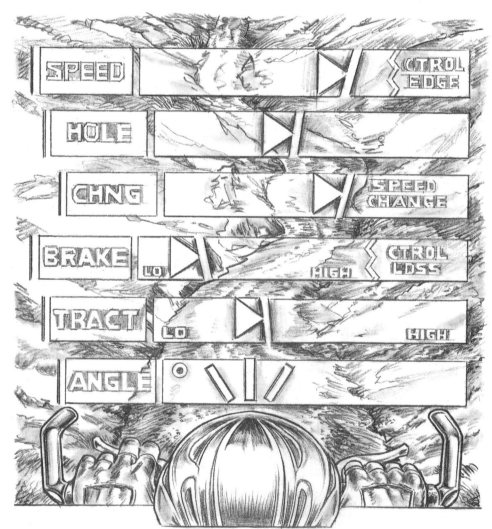

I'm getting more decisions settled before the race because it's been a disaster when I've changed them in the heat of battle.

(T&E). The second is to think through the task, then make the decision. We'll call this method **thinking it through (TIT)**. Have you ever felt forced into action and operating out of sheer panic? Take another look. The usual result of panic is **no action**. Whatever you **did do**, no matter what the outcome, was based on an earlier decision by one of the above methods.

T&E

The first method, trial and error, or T&E, depends less upon understanding and more upon practice. You don't think through the problem, just keep performing the action till it works. If the correct result is gotten, you're all right. But the drawback to making a decision strictly by T&E is that if it's changed, you must go through the whole process again to find another way.

Really good riders who learned by T&E have gone through the many possible methods of riding a bicycle so often that they can use any of them at will. They have an entire mental library of **T&E decisions** to draw on. But perhaps you don't have the time to do that.

TIT

The second method, thinking it through, or **TIT**, also has drawbacks. To arrive at a correct **decision** one must start with correct information. The rider has to be a good observer; he must review information gathered from the last ride and it has to be correct and useful information, well interpreted and correctly applied.

A wild example would be to decide to go flat out into a hairpin turn. A person who is a "thinker" probably wouldn't make such a mistake. The T&E rider, of course, would only make that mistake once.

Advised Decisions

The serious drawback to thinking it through is making decisions based upon bad information. One rider tells another to ride in a certain way and the second rider goes out and tries to fit his riding style into what he was told. If the information was accurate, there is a possibility it can work.

An example of accurate advice was when a champion rider told us the reason his standing time trial starts on the velodrome weren't smooth was because he set up his starting point with the bike pointing directly down the straight-away, into the turn. A right-handed rider should start with his left or inside foot forward. Once underway, the second pedal stroke with the right foot can deliver maximum power. Because of the banked straight-away on velodromes, the first pedal stroke with the left foot will pull the bike downward toward the infield. To counteract this he said to start with the bike pointing to the right, slightly up the banking. The combined forces of the bike pointing up the banking and his power delivery pulling it down balanced each other and he accelerated in a straight line, both smoother and faster. This was good accurate data—and it worked!

Sometimes spur-of-the-moment decisions work. I took the "guys" line at Mt. St. Ann's over a big drop-off and made it happen.

It bugs me to no end if I'm having an off day but I just stop. No reason to crash unnecessarily.

On the dark side, one rider told another that to improve his timing and control he should practice a particular descent not using his brakes at all. The first rider assured the second that there was not a turn on this descent that required braking if taken correctly. That was true, but there were also some terrific cliffs on this descent. Well, the rider tried it, made a mistake, panicked, locked up the brakes and...

A proper balance of
__Thinking It Through__ (TIT)
and __Trial and Error__ (T&E)
can eliminate many
mistakes.

Simple things like deciding
on my seat position really
work out.

Moderation

A combination of the two methods, T&E and TIT, is the best approach to decision making. T&E is time-consuming. Unless you're a full-time, team-contracted racer you probably won't have enough riding time to fully get it all. Riders who are successful through T&E only usually have had ten to twenty years of experience.

If time is a problem, every ride must count, and aside from the physical benefits, that means getting off the bike from every session with usable information for the TIT method. A clear picture of what decisions were made will be useful in the future.

T&E Only

A rider who uses the T&E method only can't work out new decisions on how to ride better and faster because he doesn't have the information neatly recorded. T&E riders face another disadvantage. Life sometimes throws upsets at us that go with us out on the bike. These upsets can consume vast quantities of attention—usually more than we can spare.

When T&E riders are upset they have an "off" day. Some things that happen can affect one's whole life, including the ability to make decisions. TIT-method riders are subject to them as well but less affected because their decisions are based on an understanding rather than a vague hope all will go well.

A good example of this contrast between the TIT method riders and the T&E type is the way in which the formerly dominant Eastern Bloc countries picked their international teams. In an effort to minimize an off day at the World Championships, personality tests were given at their selection races to help determine who would remain cool under pressure. The riders were picked not only on their riding skills but also on their ability to **think through** a potential real world riding problem, as opposed to reacting under pressure. Their programs, at all levels, were definitely TIT based.

Real World Riding

Let's look at a another real world riding decision—braking. On the road, the overuse of the rear brake is the one braking decision that commonly turns out the worst. When most riders learn to ride, they learn that the rear brake can stop the bicycle. They decide it will do that. They know the front brake will also stop the bike, but are told, "Don't use the front brake or you'll flip over." What they were told and their early experiments cause them to decide the front brake is more or less off limits for serious braking.

I switched from a T&E rider to TIT after three years. It's like hitting your head against a wall being only T&E.

T&E only is just inefficient.

Decisions can lock up a rider's ability to think. Good and bad habits come from decisions you have made about riding.

Just decide, don't waver, then stick to your decision. It's too late to worry about your tires at the start gate.

Now, the rider takes up serious cycling and is told that the front brake is as, or more important, than the rear in controlling the deceleration of a bicycle. Even so, his decisions may still find him relying on the rear brake, with poor results.

Studies of bicycle accidents in both racing and street riding have concluded that in most cases when a rider is trying to prevent an accident he uses only the rear brake. He may know the front brake will stop him much quicker but in an emergency situation returns to his original decision.

Changing Decisions

To change a decision that doesn't work and that has become a bad habit, you must go back to the original decision and **unlearn** it. Maybe "unlearn" is not correct, actually, you're making a new decision after the old one has been identified and thrown out. **You can't easily make a new decision over an old one without fully inspecting the first.** This isn't a long, drawn-out process, it can and has happened to many riders instantaneously—the bright light of understanding suddenly switches on.

Black Hole of Attention

In racing, we create an almost continuous emergency situation by pushing to our limits. Decisions on how to perform at one's limits are very important ones. Not understanding the front brake's limits, or, for that matter, the rear brake's, means you'll spend a lot of **attention** using them. It would be correct to say that indecision is the black hole that sucks up attention.

In the braking example, you may know the front brake does the best job of slowing and stopping (that decision has already been made), but you don't know at what point it can lock up and cause a crash. This creates very expensive indecision. Once a rider learns how much to apply the front and rear brakes at various speeds and loads, he can make clear-cut and inexpensive decisions under the stresses of racing. Here again, decisions pave the way for the future. **Indecision is caused by fear of the future.**

Map Trap

Another decision-making myth is that the rider can figure out his strategy and race lines by studying a course diagram. It's impossible to decide how to ride a race course, a trail or piece of road before you have actually seen it. Trying to fit a course diagram into the real world of riding will only take your attention away from good, solid observations until you've ridden it at least once.

Make It Happen

Deciding to do something is the first step to making it happen. Lots of airhead **decisions** can be made, and too many of them are confusing. Start with the most important ones first. Find reference points, points of timing; establish sub-products and products—this is your orientation process. Then decide how they fit together with the road or trail you're on. Put them together by deciding how it's going to be done, then **do it that way**. This makes a plan and provides a basis for understanding the course changes and how the race or ride may develop.

Course Walking

Deciding how to ride a course by looking it over does not always work, especially if you aren't riding it. I've had this experience with motorcycle racing and so has David with bicycles. Early in his cycling career he arrived at a race that he'd ridden for the first time a year before. This time he was much stronger and had high hopes. He got there the day before to check out the course and plan his strategy. It was roughly a two-mile circuit and he walked it to find out what could be learned. As I had in my experience, he laid on the ground and looked at each turn from the beginning, then walked through and looked at it backwards. He stood in the middle of the turns and looked at them from every vantage point possible, determined to find an "ideal" line to use through each turn.

On race day, before the race, he rode the course based on those decisions. It felt okay; he was ready to race. After the starter's pistol went off he settled into the pack, ready to make his move. He figured that when he broke clear no one would be able to stay with him because of his secret weapon—the "ideal" line. He made his breakaway all right and was really flying. He took the "ideal line" through the next turn, and then the race was over—for him.

In downhill some decisions are tough because the course can change so much from run to run: ruts, wind, rain, all have to be taken into account. That's the judgment part of it.

I do usually walk downhill courses; once when I first get there and once the night before the race.

Studying a course can help or hurt. Decisions must be based on real world conditions.

I study my problem areas and see if the course has changed, especially drop-offs.

Lesson In Ideals

His "ideal" line did not take into account one big bump and the surface traction at full race speeds. With an experience like that any smart rider would see that decisions have to be tested in actual circumstances and then compared, back to back with a stopwatch, which is what David did at the same track on another day, and he learned a valuable lesson. A combination of T&E and TIT is the key to successful riding.

You can't have one without the other, but it's important to first decide how to do it, then decide why it did or did not work. It isn't just blind experimenting, but a firm **decision** to do it one way and doing it that way no matter how it feels, then learning the results either from course times or in head-to-head competition.

Course, Lap and Section Times

Indecision slows you down.

Your times are the most reliable method of deciding what works. By recording your times on courses, trails and various sections of road you can practice a variety of techniques and determine which works. Simply decide what to do then go out and do it. This means deciding where the **points of timing, products, and reference points** are, deciding what you'll do this time out, then reviewing the times to decide if it worked or not. Did these changes improve your times? Did the times stay the same, but you found it easier to ride at this level? Both of these conclusions are valuable. **When you become comfortable with the decisions at one level of riding, you can move on to the next.**

1. Good decisions result in faster times.
2. Good times are those that improve and can be done consistently.
3. Your times are a reflection of the quality of your decisions.

This is the best way to test lines, tires and equipment—in downhill, times count.

Making full speed runs in practice can fry you. You can wind up making mistakes on race day.

Go Faster

There is, of course, a twist to the decision-making game which has to do with how powerful a decision can be. Sometimes a rider simply **decides** to go faster. He will apply this overall decision to his riding and—bang!—his times come down just like that! It can happen for many different reasons.

Watching other riders going faster can sometimes change your mind about how fast something can be ridden. You **decide** you can do it, too. Deciding to beat a faster rider can spark new life into stale riding. But, **deciding** to go faster without gaining enough experience from either T&E or TIT can get you into trouble, just like the "ideal" line escapade above.

You can see the fast line sometimes but can't hold it, or your arms get tired and you really can't hold it.

Coulda, Woulda, Shoulda

Post-race pit chatter is always interesting. New records are being set by the minute based on what the riders should have, could have or would have done. Hopes and dreams are fine, everyone should have them, except that in this case the riders are wasting those valuable moments of extreme clarity that occur after every race, where bravery, skill and technique seem totally within reach simply by deciding.

You may very well should-have-done something different, but what **decisions** would need to be made to get there? What **decisions** were made that kept you from getting there? Going fast before you're ready is scary before enough experience is gained from practice to back it up. Use those moments of clarity to decide where to pick up those split seconds. **Work out the decisions that will back up an overall decision to go faster.**

Classic mid-race decisions that usually work out badly are: "I'm going to out-brake that guy in the last turn, no matter what," or "I'm going to be the last one to stop pedaling before that last turn." Pre-race ones like the ideal line plan earlier did not work for basically the same reason—not applying the proper balance of T&E and TIT method to back up the decisions.

Past Decisions

To ride a bicycle well, you'll draw mainly on past decisions, and somewhat less on the ability to make decisions in the present. This is obvious when you consider the fact that the average amateur or Olympic trainee has a training to race ratio of at least ten to one of his in-saddle time. For pro roadracers that reverses. The pro must perform on demand with his portfolio of decisions. Racing four to six days a week means practice and competition merge into one.

In-saddle decisions can be simple ones, like using less rear brake to prevent excessive wheel hop while going into a turn or setting up the entry point and timing the entrance to a turn so that the weight distribution stays even, up to far more complex ones.

For example, having trouble going into turns too soon, a common error, might be based on the decision "not to go in too

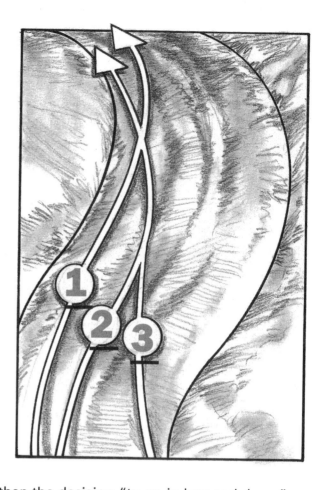

A rider's turn approach is a decision. The way you ride, in any situation, began with a decision.

high and deep," rather than the decision "to go in low and deep." This can get very tricky. The rider discovers he is always going in low, starting his turns too early, so he thinks that he has decided to go low. His real decision, way back when, was "I don't want to go in too high and deep because it's feels unsafe." So he now decides to go high and deep against that earlier decision. When he tries it he runs into his own resistance—like a mental wall. **Decisions are very powerful.**

Four-man downhill can push you into doing this. X-country can too. You see someone and go faster.

Every once in a while you might discover one of these past decisions and think, "Hey, I can do that! Whatever made me think I couldn't?" and suddenly make a great breakthrough in your riding. It is really uplifting to recognize a poor decision, instantly erase it, and put a better, more workable one in its place.

Discover Your Decisions

Here's a way to discover your decisions, whether made recently or a long time ago.

Just rely on the clock to see what is working.

1. Think over your actions on a particular turn or in a riding situation. Those that are giving you trouble should be first priority but don't ignore inspecting the ones which are going well.
2. Evaluate how well your actions work.
   a. How clear are all the steps involved in this action?
   b. What standard of performance tells you how well you're doing or going?

c. What decisions have you made to help you reach your goals?

d. What decisions are keeping you from reaching them?

3. Should you decide to:

    a. Change the decision?

    b. Not change it?

    c. Check again to see what decisions you have already made?

    d. Or, look for more information before making a new decision? In each item you come up with in numbers 1 through 3 above, you may also ask:

1. What are my **points of timing**?

2. What **reference points** did I or do I use?

3. What is my **actual product**?

4. How much **attention** am I spending?

5. How much of my **strength reserves** does it cost?

You can do this for each turn and section of a course or trail. It will take some time, and it isn't easy to do, but it will help. It's better than going slow and better than crashing.

When I see a good line by another rider I think, "Why didn't I see that?"

I write down my POTs, RPs and effort level on my course drawings from memory. Whatever I can't remember, I need to work on.

You have to find the fastest lines that won't change on you. Some riders move rocks and logs the night before a race but that makes it rough for the other riders.

The future is yours. Making decisions paves the way to predicting yourself and your performance.

The Product of Decision

By freeing up attention with clear cut decisions the door is opened to the future just a crack. In a top rider this appears to be effortless and smooth handling of situations as they occur, all the way from something simple like standing up to peddle before the hill slows your momentum, to fully "zoned out" prediction of what the other riders will do and when. The real product of your decisions is prediction.

Decision, Decisions, Decisions

The following is a partial list of decisions that could be made about using the brakes. They are not of equal importance, but each of them involves a potential decision. Take a look at each one. Consider each one by applying it to a situation you've been in. Or you can just look them over for reference and be aware of them. You may have time in the off-season to take up other aspects of riding like steering, shifting and power delivery. Break these aspects down into the decisions and actions you must make while riding.

- How many fingers to use for the front brake
- How much lever pressure it takes to lock up the front brake
- How many fingers to use for the rear brake
- How much lever pressure it takes to lock up the rear brake
- How hard you can use the front brake going into slow turns
- How hard you can use it braking into fast turns
- How hard you can use it braking into medium-speed turns
- How you can use it braking into a series of turns
- How hard you can use the rear in these same situations
- How hard you can use the brakes in the first turn of a series
- How hard you can brake going into the second turn of a series

Decisions On:

- Braking in downhill sections
- Braking in uphill sections
- Braking into a banked section
- Braking into a flat corner
- Braking into an off-camber turn
- Braking into a decreasing-radius turn
- Braking into an increasing-radius turn
- Braking into a constant-radius turn
- Braking on a smooth surface
- Braking in mud
- Braking in sand
- Braking on gravel
- Braking on a choppy surface
- Braking into right-hand turns
- Braking into left-hand turns
- Braking on crested roads & trails
- Braking in dips
- Where you should be on the course as you begin to brake
- Where you should be on the course during braking
- Where you should be on the course at the end of braking

Writing down your POT verifies a concrete starting point. If it is vague, you change run-to-run with nothing to visualize.

This information made me aware of how many decisions go into one ride or one turn.

I read through all of these and found I got a better sense of awareness from it. It forces you to address these subjects.

More Decisions

- What should you look for that tells you when to begin braking (in each kind of turn)?
- What you look for that tells you when to end the braking (in each kind of turn)? The above two questions can also be applied to particular surfaces and courses.
- Timing your braking going into slow turns
- Timing your braking going into medium-speed turns
- Timing your braking going into fast turns
- Timing your braking going into a series of turns
- Timing your braking on downhill sections
- Timing your braking on uphill sections
- Timing your braking in banked turns
- Timing your braking in flat turns
- Timing your braking in off-camber turns
- Timing your braking in decreasing-radius turns
- Timing your braking in increasing-radius turns
- Timing your braking in constant-radius turns
- Timing your braking on smooth surfaces
- Timing your braking on choppy surfaces
- Timing your braking on high traction surfaces
- Timing your braking on slippery surfaces
- Timing your braking in changing dirt conditions

Still More Decisions

- What Points of Timing or Reference Points do you use to tell if the braking is going well?
- What POT or RP do you use to decide the location of your beginning braking point?
- What POT or RP do you use to decide the location of your end braking point?
- What POT or RP do use to balance the action of both brakes?
- What information do you use to decide if the braking began early enough?
- What information do you use to decide if the braking started too late?
- What information do you use to decide if the braking started on time?
- What information do you use to determine if your front and rear brake use was balanced?

Decisions With Practice

- Braking over discolored or changing pavement surfaces
- Braking over mixed off-road surfaces
- Using the rear brake in conjunction with the front
- Using the rear brake only
- Using the front brake only
- What to do when rear end begins to hop or slide
- What to do when the front end begins to push and slide
- How to correct rear wheel hop or slide

- How to correct front wheel pushing and sliding
- How to initiate slides using the brakes in turns
- How to do it in the straights
- When to initiate these slides
- Locking up both front and rear brakes together, on straights
- Locking up both front and rear brakes together, in turns
- Body position while doing the above two
- Other people's information on the use of brakes in general
- Other people's information on the front brake
- Other people's information on the rear brake
- Other people's information on using both brakes together
- Information you got from watching other riders use their brakes
- What is useful to do with the brakes
- What is not useful to do with the brakes
- Braking when the bike is straight on various surfaces
- Braking when the bike is leaned over on various surfaces
- Braking with only the front brake while leaned over
- Braking with only the rear brake while leaned over
- How much lever pressure to use in these situations
- How far you can be leaned over and still use the brakes
- Braking and steering at the same time
- How good is your braking overall?
- How much time can be made up with the brakes?
- How much distance you can make on another rider by using your brakes?

It's good to see you are making and acting on good decisions when you see this list.

- Your seating position in all the different types of braking
- Pedaling and braking at the same time
- How slowly or quickly you can let off the front brake
- How slowly or quickly you can let off the rear brake
- How to judge your speed at the end of the braking section
- Where to position the brake levers
- How much lever play to leave
- How much stopping force the front brake has on various surfaces
- How much stopping force the rear brake has on various surfaces
- How much stopping force the front and rear brake have together
- How much the lever pressure can or must be changed while braking
- Differences in braking distance on various surfaces
- Differences in braking distance in various weather conditions: hot, cold, wet, etc.

More Decisions With Practice
- Weight distribution while braking
- Where to put your weight while braking
- Percentage of weight on the handle bars while braking
- Percentage of weight on the pedals while braking
- Percentage of weight on the saddle while braking
- These same percentages while braking, turning and leaned over
- Sitting up while braking

- Staying low while braking
- Body position in relation to wind conditions while braking
- Braking and downshifting at the same time
- Passing while using the brakes
- What happens to the steering geometry during braking (suspension bikes)
- What happens to the weight transfer during braking
- What happens to suspension during braking
- How much attention you spend beginning braking
- How much attention you spend during braking
- How much attention you spend at the end of braking
- Which is the most important part of braking: beginning, middle or end
- How much front brake can be used if the rear is locked up
- How good is your sense of traction while braking
- How good is your sense of speed while braking
- How good is your depth perception while braking
- Do you have the ability to improve your braking

Phew!!

The more you know the faster you go. *What decisions have you made about braking? What decisions have you made about riding?*

CHAPTER SEVEN

Barriers
Keys to Improvement

Depending on how a rider views it, any riding barrier either could become a big problem or it could lead to the exact solution they're seeking. A barrier is anything serving as a limitation or obstruction; a barrier obstructs but is not impassable. Let's take the simple act of turning to illustrate a potential **riding barrier**.

A common habit in steering is stiff-arming the bike and pushing it underneath in corners. It's a reaction to something the rider doesn't like and can act as a barrier to improvement.

My teammate told me not to stiff-arm the bike and it worked way better. Outside bar totally loose.

Problem/Solution

Mainly because of the top-heavy characteristic of a bicycle and the fact that a rider generally outweighs his mount by an average factor of 4:1 or more, riders can often be seen stiff-arming the bike and pushing it underneath themselves right as they initiate a turn. Some say it's because the bike feels too tall, some feel it's to compensate for that great difference in weight, some feel it will turn too fast and perhaps fall over, some are comfortable with right turns but not lefts and vice versa, some are confused about the steering process and fight the bike, and some have crashed and do it in anticipation of again being out of control.

The moment of stiffening on the bike or pushing it down to compensate for something is a common and incorrect "solution" to one of the above and is a **riding barrier**. As above, **barriers** cover a wide range of situations—from something bothersome all the way to potentially dangerous.

Riders often become gun-shy of that moment of turning-in and eventually wind up incorporating a stiffening action, or a "pushing the bike under," into their style. This could create such negative effects as adding an extra step that consumes **time** and **attention** at the turn-in-point[15]; it can promote poor handling on rough surfaces; and on slippery surfaces it may be dangerous, due to having to lean the bike over even further, making a slide even more dramatic.

Sometimes my last thoughts before a race are to relax my upper body. If I'm relaxed my prescribed lines, etc., fall into place on race day.

---

15 That point at which you begin to steer the bike in a turn.

If a rider gets the idea that, "that's just the way it is," then he's stuck with it. Feeling stuck with anything results in a problem, but a correctly identified and fully handled **barrier** will become a lasting and pivotal addition to your portfolio of skills.

Identifying that something is wrong is the first step.

Isolating it as a barrier is the second.

Solving it is the third.

Built-In Barriers

Racing and sport riding is a game where the rider need only step up his pace to find all the barriers he could ever want. Besides your physical limitations, the most obvious problem that occurs is going faster and then having **reduced time to act,** especially when it comes to cornering.

Raising the turn approach speed by only one or two mph has a remarkable effect on just about everything. Feeling rushed, a common result of this, with not enough time to act correctly, can be frustrating, yet is a fact of the game. Becoming pressed for time to

Like wind resistance, your riding barriers will increase with speed. The faster you go the less time you have.

perform in any turn is one major result of going faster. *Can you recall a time this happened?*

Time Barriers

Things do happen faster at higher speeds which, rightly, compresses the time to act and control the bike. The available time between corners, between familiar reference points, to make decisions, gear selection, braking, tactics like drafting and attacks, and of course pedaling, all change. This time-reduction and speed-increase combination acts a lot like wind resistance: the problems seem to double or triple with even small increases in speed and decreases in time to act.

Coping with speed changes will improve course times. But, having to enlist the help of adrenaline fired, panic reaction mode may gain nothing with the extra speed—except to experience what it feels like to panic.

Automatic Coach

Having less time to make decisions is not necessarily bad. In fact, whenever a rider reaches one of these time barriers, he's knocking on the door of his next area to conquer. A riding barrier is useful; it screams out the fact that new decisions are needed, or to find a better technique or focus the workouts—**it's your automatic coach**. They are also like the warning lights on the dashboard of a car. If each one is handled as it appears, a more complicated problem can be avoided later. *Could you feel good about having barriers?*

Just reading this made me aware I had some barriers—then I began to identify them.

Targeted Improvement

Ideally, we'd be able to ride either a little faster with less effort or more control every time we got on the bike—and it is possible. Of course, major power gains on a day-to-day basis are unreal and, if it's really an off-day, fighting it would be a losing battle; but a **plan** which **targets** better bike handling, improved cornering speed, steering or braking is realistic and attainable, every ride. Good riders already do this to some degree or they would not be good. Any target, no matter how simple, is better than no target at all.

You should have a plan every ride even if it's a recovery ride.

Plateaus

Something which plagues riders now and then is reaching a plateau of performance. Nothing is more frustrating than this type of barrier. It prompts a rider to go off searching for answers and often sends him on the proverbial wild goose chase to find them. These plateaus can be experienced on a daily basis but the long-term ones are the most devastating.

Dedication is one thing but butting heads with a confidence-shaking **plateau barrier**, the precise cause of which is unknown, is often a fruitless waste of time. Ironically, these performance plateaus often resolve themselves when the rider simply backs off and finds some little thing that he <u>can</u> improve. It's just a trick to gain some distance and objectivity with riding barriers, but has been known to work like a charm. *Any examples?*

I hit a plateau last year and decided to work on my starts. So BMX racing against 14 year olds was my training ground. By focusing on one thing I learned more about many things and wound up with a wicked sprint by the end of the winter.

Barriers act like physical walls. A riding plateau will often resolve itself by backing away from the problem and getting a new view of the barriers.

Physical Barriers

Most of this sport's history and written material is centered around the physical barriers: frame geometry, crank length, saddle positioning, heart rate and training, gearing, aerodynamics and so on. The physical fact of wind resistance, for example, has spawned extensive research and is something every rider is aware of. Wind resistance is ten times greater at 30 mph than at twenty, ten times greater still at 35 and ten times that at 38 MPH. No matter how aerodynamic the bike and rider are, air remains an ever-increasing barrier to speed.

Mind Barriers

I see riders write themselves off with weak excuses instead of coming up with a reason for a bad day.

These physical barriers are easy enough to recognize and do indeed point the way to areas needing work, but so-called mental barriers are our worst enemies. Mental barriers are created by riders when they sidestep or gloss over the exact, correct cause for something bad they have experienced, but these barriers are also easy to identify.

Feeling <u>distracted</u> and <u>anxious</u>, like not quite being there fully, are a drain on mental acuity. These are the warning messages in the mind's computer. The interesting thing is that many of these mental barriers can be addressed by looking at what exact skill, technique or information is misunderstood. Here are a few of the usual indicators you can look for:

    a. Being somewhat lost on the course can easily lead any rider into questioning his ability to perform or thinking his day has ended prematurely.

    b. Then too, it could be something known but not being applied, like forgetting to breathe.

    c. Simply changing gears too late, too close to the turns and crowding it with other important actions.

    d. The rear wheel may have locked up and attention is stuck on braking when it should be on turning, or braking when it should be on shifting, etc.

    e. Braking too late and losing sight of the correct turn entry speed, resulting in mild panic.

    f. The cockpit control positions on the bike may feel fine on flat sections at cruising speeds but awkward and uncomfortable under on-power racing conditions.

    g. The type of course and the road conditions may contribute to distress. For example, the entrance to a turn may be off-camber and offer less potential braking and traction than a flat surface.

All of these things can be handled by correctly identifying the exact skill, technique or information which will resolve it. That's what this book is about.

Snapping at the bike and grabbing at the controls like a shark at feeding time, is a sure sign that something isn't right. Hoping it

Every turn or section of a track has potential barriers. Find them and you can improve.

MTB riders have a bad rep for not thinking but there is strategy. It's not just a time trial.

Becoming ready for an event is different from one rider to another. Confidence comes from a sense that you will be able to overcome any barriers the ride can throw at you.

will go away the next ride or with more saddle time is optimistic but doubtful.

Other Clues

A feeling of <u>helplessness</u> and <u>disorientation</u> results from not knowing the road or trail, and can cause further problems. Not knowing where you are is equivalent to not knowing what to do.

A feeling of <u>uncertainty</u> comes from not fully understanding any riding situation. This can manifest itself in physical tension or stiffness; here again, a lack of familiar reference points is a likely cause of this, so is not trusting the front end over rough surfaces and the resulting tightness a rider experiences only serves to amplify his uncertainty. This will not only eat up attention—attention that could well be spent elsewhere for a higher return—but also physical reserves. It is another indication of a barrier.

Mistakes

This is one of the best lessons in this book. Your mistake is a result not a cause. Think about the moment before you made it.

Another great indication that all is not well is making mistakes; on the course or in the operation of the bicycle. When a mistake is made, find out where your attention was focused **just before it happened.** Look at the **decisions** and actions that lead up to the mistake—remember it's always the last thing a rider did that got him into trouble. **A mistake is a result, not a cause.**

This is the true value in knowing what was done and being able to remember it in detail. Mistakes themselves aren't all that valuable—it's in remembering what was done to bring them about which will result in improvement. A mistake isn't to be ignored in the hope it will disappear with practice—it is something to be studied and figured out. **It is a barrier, and therefore a key to improvement—_if_ handled correctly.**

Speed Errors

Riders often think that their small errors will vanish and smooth out by increasing speed. However, once they step up the pace and see another barrier, they "go off" trying to handle it as though it were a new and different one. The original problem is now masked and the can of worms is opened.

Not understanding counter-steering (fully covered later) is a good example. Without this data a rider may not be able to do the steering quick enough to match the new, higher entry speed; he runs wide and decides it was too fast when it really wasn't. Now there would be five choices:

1. Be brave and continue to make the error.
2. Become frustrated and give up by reducing speed.
3. Work on steering the bike more quickly.
4. Berserk it because the other riders can do it.
5. Ignore it and hope it goes away.

Barrier Breakdown

Overcoming barriers is not impossible but it does take some work. Do the mental part of the work as soon as possible after getting off the bike from practice or a race. First, draw a picture of each turn or section. Next, go through them, marking down the spots where difficulties were encountered mistakes were being made. (This is a far more productive alternative than sitting around pit racing.)

Close your eyes and go over these sections in your mind as you try to find the problem areas, using the procedure in the chapter "What You See." As you're studying the course from memory, some parts will be foggy, unclear or just not there. Mark these spots down on your section diagrams. Go over the entire course or

There are a lot of pros who don't ponder barriers, decisions or mistakes— off the bike is social hour.

Most riders blame their bike for their own problem areas. It's become fashionable to fixate on your bike.

Look over your mental recordings of specific sections of the course for these seven indications of problem areas.
1. Mistakes. 2. Feeling helpless or like you can't do it. 3. Pressed for time to act. 4. Doing nothing, waiting for something to happen. 5. Can't get a clear picture of some turn or area. 6. Attention stuck on some part of the course. 7. Attention stuck on something you did.

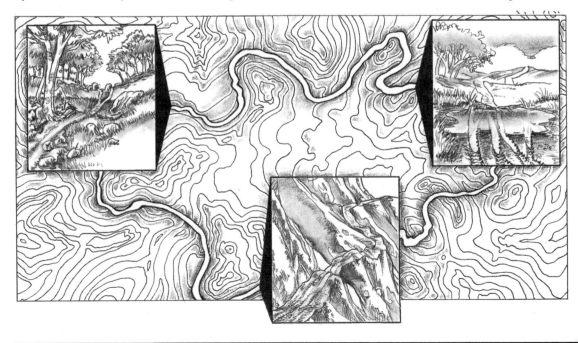

trail by memory and mark all the places that are difficult for you. Check for uncertainty, rushed time, mistakes or another of the above mentioned indicators of a **barrier**.

This simple think-it-through method can be used for solving the physical barriers to power delivery as well. Recall any fatigue-related changes in pedaling technique and on what sections of the course they occurred. Say you found yourself winded or spun out in a gear; go back to what happened a mile or a lap previously and it may be, as above, that you really were holding your breath or had **attention** stuck on something, causing the power delivery to fall apart.

Distractions Can Be Barriers

Every little thing that distracts a rider isn't a barrier; some things are just distractions, but can still inhale attention and, if left untended, become barriers. Here are some classic examples.

Speedometers—When overused, they can prevent riders from improving their **sense of speed** and can rob their attention account if they keep looking at them.

Flashy clothing—This may sound odd but a rider may be trying to live up to the image he's wearing, placing unnecessary pressure on himself to perform with everyone looking.

Pre-race chit chat—Talking about how well they'll do or how hard they've been training can create pressure, just like the flashy clothes.

Butterflies—That pre-race chitchat often comes from nervousness. For some, butterflies are so distracting they blow it before the start. But, that's racing. Without some anticipation, a

challenging ride wouldn't be exciting. Harnessing the butterflies and turning them into performance is a trick of the trade.

Equipment—Are equipment choices based on what is suitable for the course or are they just the latest goods? Gears can be too big but the rider wants to appear strong. Picking tires that are too skinny or too fat for the particular course situation because they're fashionable.

Barriers Change

Once all the apparent barriers have been listed, go back over them, pick one and decide to handle it. As any rider goes faster, the one thing that is certain is that the barriers will change; the twist is that the same problems can occur again, even in the same section or turn at the higher speeds. *Has this ever happened to you?*

Welcome Problems

Overall, barriers are good things. They tell you automatically where your problems lie. They are saying, "This is the next area to expand into, the next level of improvement." Welcome it when something's not going right. Once a barrier is recognized, you won't have to guess what's preventing your improvement or causing premature fatigue—it will point to the exact problem. It's free instruction! *Will you remember this or just butt heads with your next barrier?*

Problems like relaxing recur. You have to go over the basics once in a while. The things which require discipline, like braking in turns, diving in too early—they come back and haunt you.

Riders don't like to work on weaknesses but they turn into your strengths once handled.

CHAPTER EIGHT

Braking
The Art of Regulating Speed

Force or Finesse

Bicycle brakes are undergoing major technological improvements and in addition, suspension components and anti-fade characteristics have rapidly evolved braking tactics right out of the stone age and placed it squarely within twenty-first century technology. An anti-lock front brake is undoubtedly on the horizon.

No other commonly used vehicle will stop as quickly as a modern racing bicycle, but the improvements are more in quality than quantity. Improved surface feel and traction feedback, along with a more progressive touch, allow today's rider to accurately adjust speed with grams of lever pressure rather than pounds. All of this adds up to consistent, no-worry braking which conserves your most valued asset, **attention**. Clearing up the exact purpose of braking will save even more.

The Purpose of Braking

Even low-tech brakes are strong enough to lock up the wheel. The technology has mainly improved rider feel and anti-fade. But the main use of the brake is to gain speed, not reduce it.

The purpose of the brakes is to **adjust and correct** the speed of the bicycle downward, controlling deceleration. You know how sensitive the bike is to power input; forward speed can be adjusted in fractions of miles per hour. Going into a turn, changes in deceleration can be made just as accurately as acceleration with a correct application of the brakes.

Unfortunately, riders often have the idea that brakes are

Brakes are a big help in getting through the turns when used correctly.

some kind of on/off switch. They reach their braking point and pull them on—get down to another RP and let them off. This isn't true. You can't use brakes like that and expect to improve riding. That's asking too much of yourself.

The purpose of brakes is to **adjust** the speed downward; the overall purpose in racing is **to get around the course a little quicker than everyone else**. Considering the brakes to be an instrument to gain speed rather than lose it is the first step. No physical exercise is required—but some practice and understanding is.

Late braking often does more harm than good to corner speeds. Set comfortable brake points for yourself.

Faster Times

What part could brakes play in producing faster lap and course times without relying on consumable and limited muscular strength? On a 1 1/2 mile course with a 30 mph average speed you'll need to go about 1/4 mph faster around the whole course for a one and one half second better lap time, over ten bike lengths. Averaging one mph faster would give a six second improvement, almost a football field!

Note: Since it is impractical to look at your speeds at the entrance to every corner, let alone remember the speed you entered each one, you must rely on your <u>sense of speed</u> to know if it's faster, slower or the same as before.

To me, now, it's more of a sin to go in too slow than too fast. But, getting the speed perfect is the real challenge.

Except in downhill and other point-to-point races, maintaining a higher average speed for a whole lap, let alone a whole race, may be out of the question physically, but an increase in cornering speed for most riders is not. By going through the turns one mph faster, exits and straightaways will be both faster and easier.

You have to adjust the speed of your bike <u>accurately</u> to go around the turns something like one mph faster. How difficult is it to judge that sense of one mph accurately with the bike pitching forward and bouncing over ripples and bumps as you also try to compensate for the other riders if it's pack racing?

On downhill it's more complicated to judge turn speed because you might be sliding both ends going in.

Reverse Speed Dial

Brakes are not an on/off switch or an anchor. They are a very accurate reverse speed control. "Dialing in" the precise amount of

speed for the turn is <u>at least</u> as technical as correct gear selection. **The speed that remains when you release the brakes is the speed with which you will enter the turn.**

Everyone is limited in power so you've got to be able to go into and through the turns faster, if you want lap times to improve quickly. This is an area to find that extra speed with **no additional power output**.

Making up speed mid-turn is impractical. Pedal clearance and traction considerations take precedence over any desire to increase it. Unless it is a downhill turn, riders must set up right at the beginning for a faster entry and corner speed. **Consider the brakes to be an important tool for increasing turn speed.**

Weight Factor

The single most important factor to be aware of in braking is the weight transfer that occurs when the brakes are applied. Let's say you are a 160-pound rider and you have a 20-pound bike. During neutral acceleration with even pedal speed and flat surface conditions, weight distribution at the wheels is roughly forty-five percent front and fifty-five percent rear. A routine, non-aggressive, brake application transfers about seventy-five percent to the front wheel, leaving around twenty-five percent on the rear. The front end now weighs three times what the rear does.

At racing speeds, weight transfer from the increased stopping force is greater still: ninety percent or more of the weight can transfer to the front, leaving ten percent or less remaining on the rear. The rear tire, at the ground, now weighs eighteen pounds or less! Obviously, the rear brake can only slow or stop eighteen pounds worth of you and your bicycle. The lion's share of the braking (162 pounds) can only be done with the front binder.

While the front brake is trying to stop the wheel from turning, the rest of the bike and your body become a satellite to the front wheel and attempt to rotate around it, which is exactly what happens when you do a front wheelie. The taller your weight is on the bike the more easily it lifts the rear end. **Getting weight off the bars, towards the rear or onto the pedals, as much as possible, reduces the tendency to lift the rear wheel.**

Racing bicycles are so light that they can easily be flipped

Braking forces are awesome. A top racer can accelerate from 0 to 40 in roughly 20 seconds, his brakes will bring him back to 0 in close to 4 seconds.

When you get the entry speed just right you aren't tense. It's hard to be committed to a turn when the speed is too high.

Like before, keeping your weight back allows more stability under braking.

over under certain conditions. Hard braking over bumps and rippling pavement can launch the rear end off the ground and the net result is air between the tire and the road—a very poor traction and control situation.

Rear Brake Overuse

Overusing the rear brake is so common as to be almost a fact of life. On the road, many riders have essentially given up using it for really hard braking. It requires maximum attention, especially when it causes the rear end to hop or slide.

You can use the rear brake to test traction before going into a turn.

On the road, both sliding and hopping render the bike out of control. You can't feel good about leaning into a turn if you are basically out of control with one of the two points of contact with earth gone. Even in the dirt, a locked rear can be and often is overused as a tool for slowing and positioning the bike for a turn. Basically, you are stuck on a sliding mass of meat and metal that only wants to go straight—probably straight into what the rider didn't want to hit! The front is where the weight and stopping power are—not the rear.

Of course, in wet and slippery conditions too much front brake could cause a locked front wheel and a crash and in wet conditions must be used more gently which also allows you to use more rear.

A Bit Backwards

The use of the rear brake requires some backward logic. It seems logical to use the brakes hardest at the beginning of the braking action, when going the fastest. This is true for the front brake. In the back, however, use the lightest rear brake at the beginning of the braking action when the weight transfer is the greatest. As the front brake is released, some of the weight transfers back to the rear wheel where it can do more work. While it is true that for most riders a bicycle will come to a full stop quicker with both brakes applied, in racing, it is extremely rare that you come to a full

With your rear brake locked, the bike tends to go wide in a turn. It's still a good turn entry and positioning technique if not overused.

stop before you are done. You have to get smart with your right hand if you want to make effective use of the rear brake under racing conditions on the road.

In-turn Brakes

In-turn brakes is for emergencies like cliffs but it's a last resort.

Everyone has used the front brake in a turn before and most bikes have a tendency to stand up when the brake is applied in this fashion. While it is true that you should avoid using the brake once settled into a turn, there are exceptions (like emergencies) where it is necessary.

Crashes often occur when the rider leaves the bike at a steep lean angle or tries to hold it tight in the turn while braking. **Gradually applying the front brake while simultaneously bringing the bike upright** is the correct procedure for emergency-in-turn braking. Being stuck with a big handful of brake while well leaned over in a turn is the least attractive of the possible scenarios.

Braking after you are in a turn is an error but sometimes necessary. What is the right way to do it?

In the Dirt

In good traction you can move forward on the bike.

Off road, the braking situation is somewhat reversed. In most cornering situations on the dirt, breaking rear wheel traction to slide is an option, both as a means of positioning the bike and of slowing it. Front wheel traction is limited by the inherently slippery nature of dirt and may cause an unwanted "push" or slide with even the lightest front braking. Front slides are extremely distracting. Heavy use of the front brake in good, moist dirt traction conditions works fine. **In any conditions, the more vertical the bike the heavier the front brake can be used.**

Some feathering[15] can be used in the turns if necessary, but really should be limited to the straight-aways. In turn braking is usually a panic reaction and the speed is <u>not</u> recoverable.

---

15 Light use of the brake, "using it with a feather."

Significant Improvements

You can't make significant time improvements by using the brakes later and harder but you can by adjusting the cornering speeds accurately.

Where and how the brakes are let off is much more important than where to pull them on, as this is what sets the cornering speed. You can dive into a 20 mph turn ten feet deeper before braking than the last time and not significantly improve your lap time. Even going twenty to fifty feet deeper would gain only a few hundredths of a second per lap.

Most likely however, going in that much deeper and having to brake that much harder just might permanently enlarge your eyeballs. It always increases the possibility of costly errors like being way off line, locking the wheels, missing a gear change and so on—overspending your ten dollar bill when that attention might be better spent elsewhere, on the correct turn entry speed.

Overcompensation

By going in too deep and upsetting yourself you make it more difficult to judge the speed. **Riders tend to overcompensate for late braking by entering the turns even slower than usual.** By beginning the braking action at a comfortable location and setting the speed for the turn correctly, each turn becomes an opportunity to pick up time!

From a training perspective, it is better to back off on the initial braking marker and allow for more time to correctly set the speed than to panic with late braking. Resist the temptation to late brake in favor of getting the entry speed correct.

Try for an absolute latest braking point in training so you'll know where you'll wind up on the course when late braking is required for a passing situation.

Calculate The Brake

Looking at late braking from the standpoint of course times and your position in the race relative to the other riders clears up this point. If you're almost as fast as another rider then perhaps the few tenths gained around the whole course can really do some good. But if more than this is needed to get up to competitive speeds, don't look for it with the brakes alone; your average speed on the course will have to improve. Compare your times with the competition's and decide whether or not late braking is the answer to those seconds.

The Product of Braking

The real product of braking is **to set the speed correctly so no further changes are necessary.** If you go in too fast and require more braking when you should be turning, it can throw the timing off. If you go in too slowly you will lose your position in the turn and have to play catch-up at the exit, expending greater effort. A few turns like this and legs feel like lead. Hero going in—squid coming out.

When the front pushes you just let off the brake and turn out the bars to correct it.

Late braking is the single reason I broke bones as a beginner.

Your turn entry speed depends entirely on how smart you are with the brakes.

Taking the time to adjust the speed with the brakes (gradually) you won't have to make any corrections and **ATTENTION** will be free to ride the turn and to read the race. That old racers' rule, "Go slow to go fast," applies here as well.

End of Braking

Having an end-of-braking marker is better than simply "braking for a turn."

Establish a reference point (RP) to <u>roughly</u> mark the spot to begin braking. Braking is a sub-product and it involves at least two points of timing (POT): one at the beginning <u>and</u> one where it will be completed. Having a good end-of-braking marker allows a rider to see in advance where he'll be finished with the brakes and allows the speed to be adjusted more easily. **It is more important to establish a marker for the end of braking than the beginning.**

Practice and race speeds are usually different. So are wet conditions. That's why an EOBM is always reliable.

A beginning brake marker is okay but there is no guarantee that you will slow down exactly the same amount each lap, especially off-road, even if you brake at the same place—things like wind conditions, average speed and fatigue levels change in racing. **An end-of-braking-marker (EOBM) will yield a more reliable constant to work from.**

Sense of Speed

Your **sense of speed** is the ability to judge whether you are riding faster, slower or the same speed as during previous trips through a turn or section. Here again, you don't need to know what the actual mph is to go faster, you simply must know what a little faster feels like. To go faster you must know what faster is. A top track pursuiter[16] must be able to judge his speed to within a tenth of a mile per hour; his speed-judging abilities are very precise but he doesn't have to contend with braking. On the road, a tenth mile per hour lower average can be the difference between getting dropped or winning the race: you'd be over five hundred feet behind in a one hour event.

---

16 One who participates in very high speed time trial-type track events.

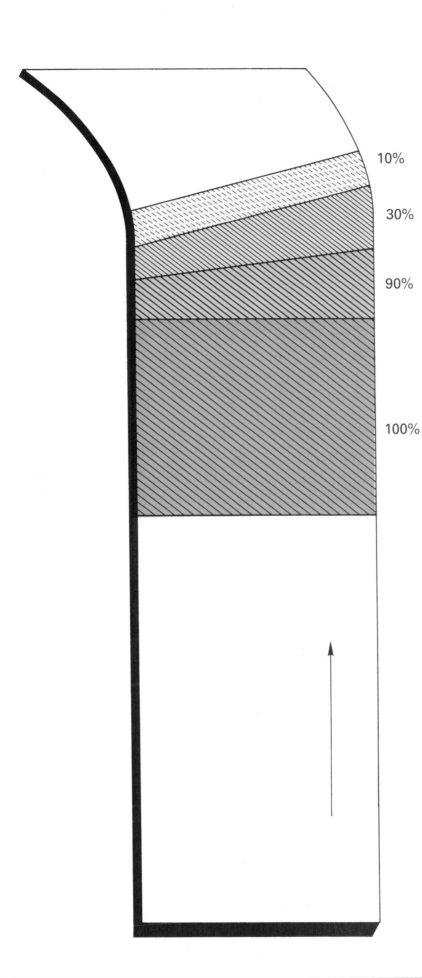

10%

30%

90%

100%

The brake is used to correctly adjust the speed for that turn. Be able to get it right each time and then work on late braking to compress the amount of time it takes.

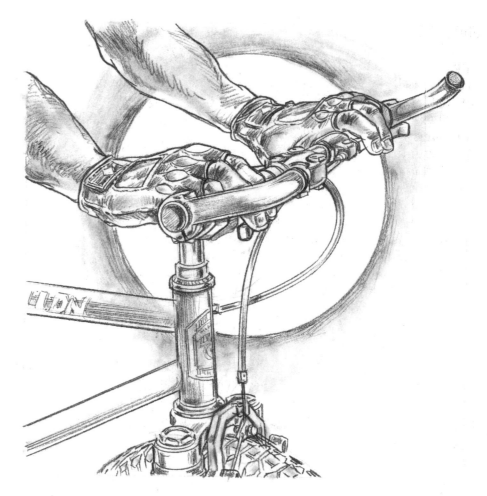

You can make accurate speed adjustments. There are two results from this:
1. You develop a better sense of speed.
2. You can spend your attention on riding the turn when you get the speed right the first time.

I'm aware of my sense of speed. You've got to know if it's right or too fast or too slow.

Plus or minus one half mph **sense of speed** gives the rider a one mph range of sensitivity. Plus or minus five mph gives up to ten mph range in **sense of speed**. That is simply too much. Five mph faster in a turn is really a great deal—enough to put you on the ground if you go for it all at once. **Here again, using the brakes as a dial makes it easier to improve your sense of speed.**

Another Twist to Braking

Another twist to braking is that you can effectively increase your speed by letting off the brakes. If you use a comfortable braking point as you enter the turn, then sense you may be going too slow, let off the brakes and maintain a speed that will be correct fifteen or more feet down the road. If the speed is set right—a little faster than the last lap— you probably won't lose as much time as you might by late braking and upsetting yourself, thereby leaving the door open for a mistake.

Braking Drills

WARNING: Two-wheeled vehicles can become extremely unstable and crash, resulting in injury, due to excessive braking. Approach these drills with caution.

It's a good idea to discover exactly what happens when the back brake is locked with the rear wheel sliding. First, get some old tires as this drill will use up the tread. Find a place with no traffic and get up to a comfortable speed—then lock up the rear brake.

NOTE: If the rear end of the bike slides out of line with the front end and you let up on the rear brake, it will (or can) **snap** back into alignment with the front wheel. If they are severely out of line, this action could be sufficiently abrupt as to damage your rear wheel or even pitch you off the bike. You can avoid this by leaving the rear brake locked until the machine is stopped, or nearly stopped, but this isn't a practical racing solution.

It is possible, with practice, to guide the wheels back into alignment with the appropriate body-english and steering corrections, then let up on the brake and continue. On asphalt, the best situation is not locking it up to begin with. Here is a drill you can practice to learn the lockup point and sensitivity of your rear brake.

Step 1: Ride along at a comfortable speed in an area with no traffic or distractions.

Step 2: Apply the front brake at a steady and even rate.

Step 3: Apply the rear brake gradually to learn how much lever pressure it really takes to lock it up.

Step 4: Repeat steps 1 through 3 until you know when the brake will lock.

Weighted Brakes

Do this drill at various speeds and with your body positioned both fore and aft over the bike. Shifts in body weight will also act as a braking assist and affect the distance of a slide. The further back and lower your body, the shorter the slide will be. Note the changes in lever pressure, remembering that the harder you use the front brake, the lighter the rear end will be and the easier it will slide.

A remarkable difference in braking occurs when riders place their weight on the pedals instead of on the seat and bars. As a drill, just ride along at a set speed with your weight on the seat and bars. Pull on the rear brake until it locks up. Next, do the same drill but with most of your weight on the pedals in the 3:00 and 9:00 o'clock positions, instead of the bars. If you don't notice a big difference in rear wheel braking efficiency, you did it wrong.

Off-road Application

Off-road riders should do the above drill to determine their braking distance while sliding. Varying the drill by intentionally keeping the back end hung out to set up a turn is called **oversteer**[17]. It simply means the rider has pointed the bike more in the direction of the turn's exit, towards the inside, without having to wait for the bike to track and steer around the turn.

While the rear end is brake-sliding to the outside the front wheel automatically steers in that direction as well. An advanced technique of forcing the bars back to a straight-on position or slightly to the inside of the turn will pivot the back of the bike towards the outside even more and quicker, but there is the risk of **high-siding**[18]. In either case, when the brake is released the rear end will hook up and go in the direction the back-end of the bike is now pointing—

---

17 Sliding the back-end to point the bike more to the inside of the turn.

18 During a slide the rider can be catapulted off the bike, towards the outside of the turn, if the tires grip too suddenly.

down the next straight section, ready to pedal, that precious moment sooner, out of the turn.

As always, the brake release should be as gradual as possible to restore traction smoothly and help avoid the snapback effect as on asphalt.

The Front Brake Drill

The purpose of this drill is to find out how much lever pressure is required to lock up the front wheel, and to experience what happens when it is locked. Without this information you'll always be afraid of the front brake to some degree. The results of this drill will differ significantly from the road to the dirt.

Off road, the front wheel will slide and turn in when locked, resulting in a crash if it turns in too far. On slippery asphalt it will do the same thing. On clean asphalt, the bike will do a stoppie. Approach this drill gradually, allowing time for your skill level to reach the performance capabilities of the brakes.

Step 1: Ride along at a slow speed, with your pedals in the 3 and 9 o'clock positions.

Step 2: Simultaneously shift your weight forward and squeeze the front brake abruptly.

Step 3: As the rear wheel comes off the ground, unlock the front brake and let the rear wheel back down.

Make sure the front brake is released gradually. If it's released like a light switch, the rear end will drop down hard,

Turn in the front creates a definite braking action. It can be dangerous.

possibly damaging the rear wheel (and your private parts as well). This is just a drill, it helps in determining the lever pressure it takes to lock it up and see how it feels. **When riding and racing, the only mistake you can make with a locked front wheel is not backing off the lever soon enough.**

Another Brake Drill

For a riders own information, he should know what the braking distances are when using just the front brake, just the rear brake and a combination of the two. Use each of the three methods to see how long it takes to stop. Just pick a constant braking point and make note of the different stopping distances. Try it on the dirt and road and even on uphill and downhill sections.

The purpose of the braking drills is to free attention and familiarize riders with the sensations of hard braking. Once there is confidence in the ability to slow and to stop the bike, you'll save big in your ATTENTION account. **There is no real magic in brakes except how you use them.**

Could you improve your braking?

CHAPTER NINE

Steering

It Happens Backwards

Every corner starts with a steering action by the rider. The purpose of steering is **to accurately control the bicycle's direction of travel**. When you consider the fact that only two things can be done with any bicycle—change its speed and change its direction—steering is fifty percent of yours and your bike's capabilities.

Riders who have felt tentative or uncertain about steering and cornering, that have a limited zone of comfort when it comes to the degree of lean angle or changing lean in turns, that sometimes find themselves "easing" into curves where pros are positive, precise and in command, know there is something to learn.

A slight pressure on the bars in the opposite direction you intend to go is COUNTER STEERING. It's how you have been doing it all along.

Counter-Steering

All single-track (one behind the other), two-wheeled vehicles steer by a process called **counter steering**. <u>Counter</u> means against, and <u>steer</u> means to guide or direct: you apply pressure to the bars in the <u>opposite direction</u> of the intended turn. You wish to go right—a slight pressure on the bars to the left makes the bike go right. You want to go left—pressure to the right makes it happen. This is how a bicycle or a motorcycle steers and it's the only way to gain pinpoint accuracy with steering.

It Does Not!

"I just lean and my bike steers," or, "I can steer without even touching the bars," are the two things that might begin the argument you will eventually have with someone who disbelieves you. Here's how to handle it. "Fine", you say, "put your arms out as though you were holding onto the bars and lean right." He'll see he is extending his right arm and contracting the left. Then say, "You've been **counter steering** all the time without knowing it." When he leans right, he pushes on that right bar, and he may also pull on the left one—same difference, it is **counter-steering**.

Blame Your Parents

These arguments come about because of a cruel trick that parents play on children. They buy them tricycles before bikes and tricycles steer right to go right and left to go left. So do cars and practically everything else except rudder stick boats. When learning to ride bicycles, children are accused of having poor balance. Not true. They simply expected a turn-right-go-right and got a turn-right-go-left, then became confused and crashed! Eventually, but not necessarily with understanding, we ride.

However, the tricycle experiences can haunt one. Have you ever frozen on the bars when an unexpected pothole or car was in your path? **In a panic**, turning the bars trike-style will have the rider going exactly where he **does not** want to be. Most riders are quick to sense this error and simply freeze on the bars in confusion, often hitting the obstacle. *Would you train a child with a trike or with understanding?*

Steering vs. Leaning

Another confusion brought about by parents and other riding "coaches" is the just-lean-it advice. But, don't be confused about leaning and steering, they are <u>not</u> the same thing. This can easily be illustrated by riding along in a straight line and pushing the bike down and away from you. An absolutely straight path of travel can be maintained while the bike is leaned over quite far. **Leaning does not always equal steering.**

Overcoming the Forces

When spinning, the wheels of your bicycle create **gyroscopic force**. That is the resistance felt when you attempt to tilt a spinning bicycle wheel held firmly in your hands by the

axle ends: it first resists your attempt and then goes off in a seemingly unpredictable direction where it will stabilize if you don't try to tilt it again. The faster the wheel is spun the more stability it gains. A spinning gyro will stabilize in any position if no additional outside force is applied, just like the toy gyroscopes you spin by pulling a string.

The two **wheel gyros** of a bike create its stability and tendency to continue going straight. The **counter steering** process upsets the front wheel's gyro effect and helps lean the bike and you over at an angle. However, even when there is some pressure being applied on the bars in the opposite direction, **the front wheel angles in to the turn**. The further you steer the bike to steeper lean angles, the more the front wheel turns in to the turn to achieve the desired turning radius.

Stop and Stand Up

To stop the counter-steering/leaning process one only has to relax his pressure on the bars and the bike will stay at that lean angle with either no or very little further assistance from the rider. The wheel gyros stabilize it in that position—only provided they maintain enough speed. If the speed drops, the bike will tend to "stand up" as there is not enough gyro effect to hold the lean angle against the outward bound cornering force. Weight transferring to the front wheel from deceleration also adds to the bike's tendency to "stand up." At slower speeds it's the opposite, the bike tends to fall inward.

The faster you go, the more precise your steering must be. Products, sub-products, points of timing all become useable with accurate steering.

In-Turn Turning

Once in a turn, to alter the lean/turn radius again, a further pressure on the bars is needed to "upset" the newly achieved stability, always in the opposite direction of the intended turn. And always, the faster you go, the more bar pressure is needed to overcome the gyro effect. For example, under high-banked velo-drome circumstances, you may find yourself having to both push **and** pull to overcome the combined gyro and G-force loads imposed on the bike.

Steering Confusion

Engineers often disagree with one another on the gyro effect theory, but there is good evidence that it is at least partly correct. The rider of an over-300 mph record-attempt motorcycle observed that the machine **counter steered** at speeds up to 225 mph—and **then reversed** to car type steering. He then said **it reversed again at about 275 mph**, returning to counter-steering. Imagine being confused at that speed!

This phenomena known as counter steering is best and most easily observed at speeds above fifteen mph where the light wheels

Counter-steering applies in all situations. Even when already banked over, you must counter steer again to increase lean and tighten your turning radius.

can create enough gyro force to clearly feel the effect. At lower speeds it still works this way but is sometimes difficult to observe, mainly because the steering on most bikes is so light and sensitive that they seem to turn by intention alone. NOTE: when balanced, stopped or nearly so, you can actually turn the bars like a trike.

Weight Shift Steering

It is true that by shifting your body's weight the bike can be coaxed into a sort of vague turning; "hands off the bars" riding will tell anyone that is true. But this isn't what we call steering, this is simply overwhelming the gyro effect with your superior and very influential top-heavy mass.

Counter-Flick

Hands-off-the-bars steering is most easily accomplished by leaning your body in the desired direction and flicking the bike (using your seat and pedals as pivot points) in the opposite direction of your intended turn. It isn't either accurate or quick enough for precision cornering, pack maneuvering or obstacle avoidance, but is a modified version of counter-steering.

Tighten the Turn

To increase the lean angle, which must be done to "tighten up" any turn, you'll need to counter steer again. A fast decreasing-radius turn is a good example. More lean is often needed toward the end of it and a rider can be seen trying to force the bars in the direction of the turn, trike style, but it doesn't work. Now he is ripe for a mistake and will generally lose speed and become rigid as the bike goes toward the outside of the turn. In such a situation, a rider may think he's going too fast for the turn, but actually it's just too fast for their steering technique.

Most steering correctly occurs with the original steering action going into the turn, but tactical and hazard avoidance corrections are often necessary. If a rider can't **quickly and accurately** correct the steering in a turn, he'll limit himself by a "one line through the turn" approach; in pack riding this is an unworkable situation.

Perfect Panic

Racing is a very satisfying emergency condition. Panic is an unsatisfactory condition where one's <u>attention</u> becomes fixated and locked. The fact that a rider may freeze or turn the bike trike style answers many a question about why he went into the curb or ditch or hit that pothole.

Because of its backward nature, counter-steering your bike in a practiced and positive manner can shorten those moments of panic down to an acceptable level and allows the freedom to completely control the bike's direction.

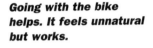

Going with the bike helps. It feels unnatural but works.

Slide-Steering

It's not the bicycle that causes a little slide to evolve into a crash; most of the time it's the rider. The nature of a bicycle is stability. In fact, as above, during any rear-end slide, your bike will automatically point the front wheel, perfectly, in the right direction to compensate for that slide—it steers itself!

Any rider who is tight on the bars in a slide, not allowing the bike to stabilize itself, or is trying to correct the slide with too much force, instantly makes it worse. Steering it in, or simply holding on too tight, makes the front grab and may cause a high-side, while steering it out increases lean angle, making it slide even more.

Slide-steering is a delicate business, requiring very little, if any, rider intervention. It requires none if a rider is

Pushing the bike underneath your body for cornering feels right for control but has two disadvantages.
1. You have to lean it over further, and 2. Being stiff on the bike creates handling problems.

trying to ride out the slide and very little if he's trying to guide it.

As noted before: There is a high-level, creative side to slide-steering in the dirt where you take these two aspects and make them work for you. Turning the bars in and purposely making the front end bite will help slow the bike and can act as a pivot for bringing the back end around at low speeds.

Go With It

For sliding in the dirt, pushing the bike under gives more control. Push it under more and slide more. Pick it up and slide less. However, for high traction conditions and especially for the road, it is counterproductive in two important ways.

1. While pushing the bike under maintains the body in a more straight-up-and-down balance, an "in alignment with gravity" position, it also requires more lean angle to negotiate the turn; **the bike must be leaned over further to compensate for the rider's more vertical position**.

2. Because it sets the rider in a stiff-arm to the bars position, it can make the bike overreact to any body motion,

Going with the bike accomplishes the most turning with the least leaning.

bumps or uneven riding surfaces. **Going with the bike, in alignment with its lean angle, solves these two problems before they even start.**

Quick Review

1. As long as you continue **counter-steering** by pushing and/or pulling on the bars the bike will continue to lean over and turn more sharply.

2. When you ease the pressure on the bars the bike will stay

at the lean angle you've achieved, providing only that you've maintained the speed necessary for that lean angle.

3. You don't have to hold the bike into the turn with any great amount of force, if at all—the gyro effect of the wheels holds it there.

4. In a slide, the bike will self correct the front wheel's direction to stabilize itself.

5. To tighten your turning radius in any turn you must counter steer again.

6. Going with the bike (instead of pushing it underneath) reduces the amount of lean angle you need to negotiate a curve.

Learn To Turn!

CHAPTER TEN

Turn Points
Point Of Entry

Everyone has a turn-in or turn entry point—it's where the steering action for any turn or corner is begun. Whether the turn-in point is consciously selected or not is the question. A predetermined turn entry point is one of the most important **decisions** for any corner. It is a key **sub-product** and affects the **timing** and execution of eleven important riding tasks.

1. How fast the turn is approached
2. Where the brakes go on
3. Where the brakes go off
4. Where you stop pedaling
5. Where you change gears
6. How quickly or slowly you will have to steer the bike
7. How much lean angle you will use
8. Where the bike is pointed once fully leaned over
9. How many (if any) steering corrections you will make
10. Where you will finish the turn (how wide you run at the exit)
11. How early you can start your turn exit power delivery?

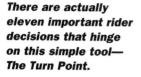

There are actually eleven important rider decisions that hinge on this simple tool— The Turn Point.

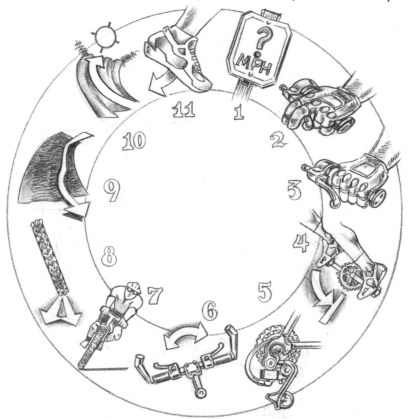

Turn Point Tool

Are these eleven decisions/actions important? Take a simple thing, like gear changing; say you waited too late to do it. Would that crowd the actions of getting off the brakes and steering? It could. Would having a turn point give an exact idea of when the shifting should be completed? It would clear it up. Everyone has some sense of their intention to turn the bike; it's not anything new, but is often taken for granted as "just part of riding." A pre-selected turn point is a **tool** which gives any rider an exact reference point to adjust all eleven of the above.

Turn points are critical in places like crested corners that turn on the downside. Too early and you slow down too much, too late and you are light.

The most obvious result of your turn entry point is where you will wind up at the exit. Choose wisely and you own the turn.

Command Point

Either you are in command of the turn or it is in command of you. There isn't much middle ground. Take a series of turns as an example. A too-low turn point on the entry usually creates problems (too wide) at the exit of the second or third corner; the turns are in command. By selecting a different turn point you can reverse that situation the next time through.

I pick alternate turn points for possible changing conditions. They are going to change for wet or dry.

Traffic and Mistakes

Pack riding, passing and mistakes may alter a turn point for a tactical advantage. Examples:

1. You might treat another rider's position as a DR turn if you were planning a turn exit attack.

2. You may enter low to block an entry pass.

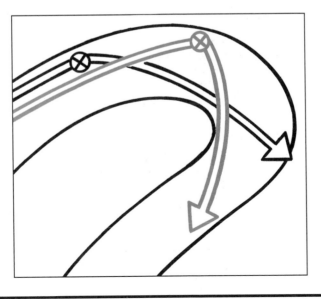

Correctly adjusting a DR turn is done with your turn-entry-point tool.

Be advised, the rider who has a consciously selected turn point knows where he is and the rider who doesn't is lost to some degree. Missing a turn point gives immediate knowledge that more of the above eleven will change <u>before</u> you are forced into additional, often costly, corrections.

Sharpen the Tool

A turn point is a tool that, like any other, requires practice. Recreational riders are faced with these same eleven riding tasks. The easy flow of normal riding provides an excellent training format for finding and using turn points: there is no reason why riding should not be accurate at all speeds. If a rider can't find turn points and use them at lower speeds, it's unlikely they'll magically appear when needed at racing speeds.

Wrong Is Right

Each of the eleven tasks listed above can consume attention or sap strength from errors connected with them. Having and using turn points frees up attention—you are able to think ahead by locating the most important point of timing there is. It's not really important whether the exact right turn-in point is established or not. Having the "wrong" turn-point is better than not having one at all. It will still free up attention. *Every corner has a turn point.*

Point of Entry

It's hard to discipline yourself to go in late and wide even if you know its a DR turn and you really will go faster.

Considering your end product can have a precise location on the course or trail, so should the beginning point—the two are connected. Taken by itself, the point of entry is where the major steering change occurs for the turn. This is a sub-product. In banked turns, the entry point should always be designed to use the banking to the best advantage and be gauged by the exit product. The emphasis is to use the banking to your advantage. This same concept applies to off-camber, DR, IR—any type of turn. You can think of it as "connect-the-dot" riding.

Going in to turns too soon commits you to one speed and lean angle for a greater portion of the turn, which leaves you fewer options for corrections, and makes riders feel they can't or shouldn't make any changes in their line. The result is that maintaining traction, passing, steering, shifting gears and pedaling out of the turn all become matters of great

Having a good sense of what you are trying to achieve in a turn, the product, provides all the information needed to choose an accurate turn point.

concern and more difficult to do smoothly. Going in to turns too soon is an indicator that you do not have your product well defined, that you're slightly lost. **Not knowing where you're going in a turn invites you to enter it too soon.**

Faster Is Deeper

Here's another way of looking at it: if you make your major steering change at the same point going into a turn yet, because of higher entrance speeds, carry more speed, you will run wider than your last pass through—you may believe you went too fast for the turn.

In loose hairpins sometimes it's faster to go in sliding the back around to tighten the turn.

One remedy for this is to go in **later** (wait longer to turn the bike) before making the steering change. The major, and often difficult requirement is that you turn the bike quicker at your new turn point; but it will straighten out the exit. **The earlier you wish to begin your exit pedaling in a turn, the later you have to set your turn point.**

Patience can make a huge difference in exit drive.

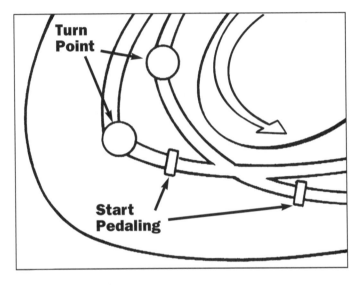

In the dirt, the same result can be gotten by squaring-off the turn, sliding the back end around and making it oversteer—that costs speed. You have to decide if it is affordable or not.

Go Fast, Slow

Going in deeper and faster, means the steering change will need to be even more abrupt, and the bike will not want to turn as easily as before. One trick to going in later is to go a bit slower, feathering the brakes to your turn point. This requires some restraint but, as many champions say, "Learn to go slow to go fast."

There is a law of diminishing return on late turn points. Waiting too long to turn will force you to slow and lose too much turn entry speed; but don't give up if it doesn't work the first time; this is a useful tool and the main point is knowing where you went into the turn so that there is something to change and adjust.

Having and using a turn point is vital to any rider who desires more control over his cornering.

CHAPTER ELEVEN

Sponsorship

There Is No Free Lunch

I'll get to the nitty of sponsorship right away: You need one of three things—or all three—to get sponsorship support.
1. Know someone who is in a position to sponsor you.
2. Work hard promoting yourself and cover every possible sponsor.
3. Be so good at racing that other people want you on their team carrying their stickers and colors.

What is it worth? In a shot like this, you win, your sponsors win and the magazine who prints it wins too.

A P.R. World

I have to meet the real person: I have to like them and their product.

In most cases, people want to sponsor riders they like or ones the fans do. Sometimes, that's more important than the ability to ride, but usually it just helps a lot. A potential sponsor may picture his rider on the winner's stand or on TV at the Tour de France or at Mammoth saying great things about him. He may just picture them at the local events promoting his product to others. Are you the kind of person that others believe?

Your sponsor—or potential sponsor—must understand one thing if he is to be at all successful. **We live in a PR (Public Relations) world and good PR helps.** If any rider just expects to

Along with your wins comes status. People want to know what you think. What you say can be valuable, $$$.

be a local racer and nothing further, this doesn't exclude him from the fruits of sponsorship. Local racing has been the spawning ground for some of the most successful product lines ever. *Have you noticed this?*

His Honor, The Racer

Racers are opinion leaders in their fields. This field is bicycling. Throughout racing history, the majority of products that are sport or performance-related have shown up on the race track, then on many production bikes.

If you have raced and have friends, you probably noticed that your credibility has increased among them. Your friends and their friends are depending on you to give them the hot tip on performance parts and even on what bike to buy.

An opinion leader is somewhat of a celebrity. You, as a racer, must fulfill the requirements of a celebrity. If you have any success in racing, be willing to answer endless questions about bicycles. A sponsor should understand that you are willing to promote his products. When you are a great racer, nobody will expect you to do any of this because you will have become overpaid and cocky. Not really—but the winning will be first priority.

The basis for sponsorship, whether you are a top racer or not, is the exchange you can make with the sponsor. What can you do for him and what is he going to do for you?

Step One is getting the sponsor. Step Two is spreading his name around. Step Three is win, win. win.

Decide, Plan and Do!

It's up to you to decide upon and sell to your potential sponsor the exact plan for getting his name out into the world in the best possible light. Plan for activities such as arranging for articles, making your pit area into a sort of mini trade show for his products, showing him that you have a sphere of influence, pointing out that racing is and has been good promotion, and anything else you can dream up to show him how it will benefit him. Then do it!

Keep a sponsor informed of what you're doing, or propose that you will inform him. Take pictures, write letters and keep him up to date. *Can you do it?*

Proposals

Proposals should be well-organized and look professional. If you outline a great season of promotion and show up with a dirty or disorganized proposal, he will see through it from the start. He won't be confident that you are the conscientious, well-organized person he needs to do the job. Begin to think of yourself as an employee of a company in which you own shares of stock.

Promises, Promises

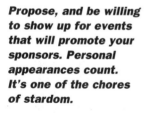

Don't start by going for the money.

Don't promise anything that can't be delivered. Think out the year ahead and write up a plan which can actually be carried out. The number of companies that will pay to run stickers at the amateur level is dwindling and has almost disappeared. Don't base a sponsorship package on the fact you will run his stickers on your bike and shirt. Too many riders will run stickers for a set of tires or just for fun. Design the package so it will stand on its own whether there are stickers on the bike or not. Propose to make yourself available for promotional activities, trade shows, and so on. *Any thoughts on this?*

Propose, and be willing to show up for events that will promote your sponsors. Personal appearances count. It's one of the chores of stardom.

The Year Ahead

The most important part of any sponsorship package is one that sponsors and riders must both be well aware of. I have seen it overlooked countless times with unfortunate results.

In the Fall of the year companies are looking around to see how they will spend their promotion dollars. They are enthusiastic and expect that the coming year will be good. They have dollars that they feel compelled to spend on promotion. The advertising people are pumping them up for the coming season. It is winter and the grass will be greener in the spring.

You go in with a good proposal and everything looks right. You're pumped, the company is going to give you $500 and all the product you can use. It will be a help. The season begins and you go about promoting the product as agreed. When the season ends, you go back to your sponsor to see about next year and he says, "What did you do for me this year?" You talked up the product and spent a lot of time keeping up your commitment, but now it all slips away from you and it seems petty to mention each time you talked to a group of riders on the Sunday ride to pump his product, each time you carefully placed stickers on the john walls, every time you got someone to believe in the product.

Here's the Deal

If the sponsor spends money on a sponsorship, he had better be willing to spend more money telling people about it. Sponsorship is a two-way street. You don't get something for nothing and neither does he. It takes an effort on both parts to get

You really are in a partnership with your sponsors.

Your sponsors must realize that money and product is not PR. You are working hard, they have to make an effort too.

the word out. On the local level he should be supplying you with banners and pins and stickers to give away, and maybe an ad in VeloNews to commemorate your good performance. A race program ad, for instance, helps him get his name out and also makes you better known. The sponsor builds his rider and his product at the same time.

It's a PR world, and the more they see of you and the product, the better PR it is. You've got to have the sponsor agree to back you throughout the year—win, lose or draw.

If the sponsor won't back you in this way, find another sponsor. Your guy doesn't understand what he is sponsoring you for in the first place, and you'll lose him when he loses his initial enthusiasm. At the end of the year, if he has used his resources to put you and his product out there, he won't ask you what you did for him— he will <u>know</u>.

As riders, we have to eliminate this idea that there is some kind of magic that goes along with racing. A win—or lots of wins— will not do anything for the sponsor. It will be his follow-up that gets the word out. *Do you get it?*

Your PR Program

Even without a bunch of first places you can still do plenty to make yourself known. Despite the Olympics, racing is still such an unknown quantity—in the U.S. especially—that you can promote yourself on late-night radio talk shows, public-access TV and taking part in civic-minded activities during the off-season such as talking to boys' clubs. Start a "helmet safety" or "clean up a riding trail" program that might save a life or make a racer of someone. You can of course plug your sponsor here. Local newspapers are always hungry to fill space with stories about local people. You can go into one of them with the same civic-minded approach and it would be difficult for them to turn it down. Urge other riders to do the same. It may seem you're sharing the spotlight, but in the end it makes racing more popular, which gives sponsors a better reason to participate. *Any examples?*

Satellite Sponsorship

A key target is one well-known sponsor. This allows other sponsors something to identify with, something larger to be connected with than just Joe Smith, racer. They revolve around and bask in the light of the better-known central sponsoring company. The possible advantages of being a satellite linked to a large company with a multi-million dollar advertising budget is very appealing to the smaller businessman. You are doing him a favor by linking him with a big central sponsor.

For example, when a new man is signed onto a factory team, in many cases he is still an unproven rider—high potential obviously, but he has not yet won any races. Still, a new team rider for any factory has little difficulty in finding sponsors that will pay handsomely for a patch on the jersey. The sponsor can now be

Decide what size pond you can fish for sponsors. Getting one large enough for dinner is better than none at all.

connected to the factory team and the factory advertising campaigns.

The rider, in this case, is of secondary importance. The sponsor may pay the rider $5,000.00 for placing the patch or stickers, but the factory may use photos in tens of thousands of dollars worth of ads, posters and promotional items. *Some examples?*

Big Fish

Landing a big sponsor can be useful in helping you gather satellite sponsors. Going to a big company with a small, but effective plan that will not drain the promotional budget can be of more value than going in with an expensive program that may be turned down. It is still the same idea as above. Large companies like to get bargains, too, and the smaller company feels connected. Remember, your contract terms may be kept confidential, if you choose, so the other sponsors you approach don't know whether you are getting $10,000.00 or $100.00. Keep it that way.

Where To Fish

The size of the pond you fish in for sponsors is important. A factory is a large fish in a large pond, worldwide. They have the money to buy the best. If you are not the best—yet—start fishing in a smaller pond to begin with. You may only get a shock from the local accessory store, but that now makes you appear connected to something larger. You are a satellite and revolve around the sponsor as well. If you can do a great job of promoting the shock there might be some gas money the next time you talk to the sponsor. Plaster its name over everything you can, and even spend money on your own to prime the pump. (It makes you look like you're getting more from your sponsor, and a new sponsor will expect to pay more from what he has seen in the past.) Move up the sponsor ladder one size pond at a time. You may even start in a large puddle, but at least it is wet. *Does this apply to you?*

Over the Limit

Once you begin to catch sponsors, don't go over the limit—throw back the small ones. Coming out on race day with 30 stickers—your sponsor may have to ask where his name is. Pick the best sponsor and make him the central figure, then don't crowd the space. A few sponsors, three to five, still allow everyone to get his share of exposure without feeling lost. Think of your own time also. You won't be able to do as good a job promoting 10 products as you will with only three.

That's Show Biz

Sponsorship is the business end of the racing game. It has little or nothing to do with the riding itself except for one very important thing: **Having enough money to operate your program buys time to concentrate on yourself as a rider.** Spending all your time doing your job to make money for racing can get very old, very fast. If you could spend eight hours each day on your riding skills rather than working on your bike or at the job, you would see some dramatic improvements.

When you keep your sponsors informed, they are getting an exchange from you already.

One of the original ideas of sponsorship was to let skilled artists and craftsmen have the time to create their work. Use your sponsorship to create yourself as a better rider. Treat sponsors in a businesslike and friendly manner. Increased sales is their bottom line. Keep the business separate from your riding, but don't forget that it is part of the three main factors for success. They are: Good riding, good equipment and good sponsors.

Factory Rides

Sponsorship also brings about the possibility of a factory ride. The factories, and the people they listen to, are often very good at spotting who has the potential to be a topnotch rider.

A word of caution: Even though it has become ever more popular to take drugs in this society, this is something that smart team managers are on the lookout for. Riders who have a reputation for partying are not being looked on with favor. Drugs are like a decreasing-radius turn—they fool you into going in too fast, then make it very hard for you to get out.

In closing on the subject of sponsorship, a written agreement is always in order. If you obtain sponsorship, get the terms <u>in writing</u>—at least until you see how each other operates.

And one other point, sometimes it's better to pay for supplies than to get them with invisible strings attached. Herein lies a great truth: **It often costs more to get things for free than it does to pay for them.** Keep up the agreed-upon exchange with your sponsor and it should work out fine.

From the sponsor you get money and stickers, etc. Money is payment for how well you expose the stickers and his name. *Good fishing...*